YACHTMASTER OFFSHORE

THE RYA SEAMANSHIP FOUNDATION

John Russell, the author, has very kindly given all the royalties of this book to the RYA Seamanship Foundation. The Chairman and trustees of the Foundation wish to thank the author for this generous donation which will be used to further the Foundation's work in promoting a high standard of seamanship among amateur yachtsmen.

The author's special thanks are due to Bill Anderson, Cruising Secretary of the RYA, without whose patient encouragement this book would never have been written, to Alison Eyre who gave her time and skill to the cause in deciphering the manuscript and typing it, and to Joanna Russell, his wife and sailing partner, whose comments have been seamanlike and constructive but never 'wifely'.

YACHTMASTER OFFSHORE

THE ART OF SEAMANSHIP

P 37/38
f 42

JOHN RUSSELL

Preface by James Myatt, Chairman RYA/DOT
Yachtmaster Qualification Panel

With seven drawings by Seachase and
diagrams by the author

Royal Yachting Association
in association with
David & Charles
Newton Abbot London North Pomfret (Vt) Vancouver

Author and publishers thank Laurent Giles and Partners Ltd of Lymington for the loan of the photograph of *Vertue XXXV*. They are also grateful to Westerly Marine Construction Ltd of Waterlooville, Portsmouth, for the loan of the photographs of the two Westerly boats, to Mr Alan Hollingsworth for the one of *Blue Charm* and to Mr David Burnett for those of *Ismana* and *Varangian*.

ISBN 0 7153 7465 6
Library of Congress Catalog Card Number 77–89374

First published 1977
Second impression 1978

© RYA Seamanship Foundation 1977

Printed in Great Britain
by Redwood Burn Limited Trowbridge & Esher
for David & Charles (Publishers) Limited
Brunel House Newton Abbot Devon

Published in the United States of America
by David & Charles Inc
North Pomfret Vermont 05053 USA

Published in Canada
by Douglas David & Charles Limited
1875 Welch Street North Vancouver BC

CONTENTS

PREFACE

What makes a man a competent yacht skipper? Navigational ability, skill in seamanship and competence in boat handling are the most obvious of the many qualities required. All these subjects are taught at yachtmaster certificate courses but knowledge alone does not guarantee success at sea. Efficiency as a yacht skipper calls for an element of judgement, to apply knowledge and skill to specific situations, often under tough conditions. This judgement is the essential quality which an examiner is looking for when testing a yachtmaster candidate.

In this book John Russell makes a valuable contribution to the yachtmaster ideal by identifying the many factors on which a yacht skipper's judgement is based. From his own broad experience of cruising he has drawn the essentials that make cruising under sail a fascinating and rewarding way of life. I am sure that many future yachtmasters will be inspired and helped by his work.

James Myatt
Chairman, RYA/DOT Yachtmaster Qualification Panel

INTRODUCTION:

The cruising skipper

The highest reward of all sports, even competitive ones, is the conscious savouring of perfect performance. The triumph of being first past the finishing post is transient, the faultlessly timed and co-ordinated output of the last ounce of energy into the spurt that took you there is imperishable.

As with other sports the satisfactions of cruising increase with expertise. Confident mastery brings relaxation and the calmness to relish experience; incompetence breeds anxiety, irritation, frustration and shame, so that no-one has any fun. In cruising, however, the skipper is more the leader of an expedition than the captain of a team, and his influence is paramount. A poor crew can make a successful and enjoyable cruise under a good skipper, but no matter how good the crew they will be miserable if badly led.

The professional seaman becomes the captain of a ship and assumes the responsibility and authority of his office by virtue of his training, experience and qualifications. He is supported by the Law, the habit of discipline and the hierarchy of command. He has the advantage of a precise relationship with his crew, and can expect every man to know what his job is and how to do it. It is a safe bet that the captain of a naval or merchant ship is, of all her company, the man best fitted to fill the post; the recognition of this by all hands does much to endorse his authority and lighten the burden of his responsibility.

The skipper of a yacht carries similar responsibilities. Small though his ship may be, the lives of her people are in his hands, and his mistakes can endanger other vessels as well as his own.

Yet how came he to command? What are his credentials? It may be that his training and experience are limited to a bit of reading and some unsupervised experiment, that his qualification is that he paid for the boat or fathered the bulk of his crew, and yet it may still be an undoubted fact that of all the people on board he is the one most fitted to command. Whatever the answers to these questions, his authority will stand or fall by his manifest ability to manage, handle and navigate his ship and her crew. If he really knows his job his crew will follow him devotedly and his ship obey him like a circus horse; but there can be no bluffing, for the sea is ruthless in demolishing pretences, and noisy commands may achieve no more than the advertisement of incompetence.

Despite his disadvantage compared with his professional counterpart, the amateur skipper has one enormous asset. Being his own master he has the time to experiment and practise, the freedom to arrange things so that he can make mistakes with impunity, learn from them without penalty, become wiser without being saddened in the process.

One man who understood this was the lone yachtsman who approached a pontoon on a quiet afternoon. Coming in slowly under power, he brought up in the berth, looking round reflectively as the yacht's bow paid off, juggled with tiller and engine controls to turn her round, stood off and came back again. Offers to take his lines were declined with a smile. 'I am learning to drive' he said. Not for him the searing experience of discovering, in a crowded harbour and force six, that he has lost way too soon, his fenders are bunched too much amidships and the throttle is up his trouser leg.

One who did not understand was an owner who invariably went in and out of harbour under his auxiliary. When it failed to start in the approach he naturally had to sail in, and having never done this before he not only lacked a precise knowledge of the way his boat would respond, but was totally unprepared for the problems that would confront him. As the yacht beat in, anxiety and tension were evident in the helmsman's rigid stance, the many shouted orders that were often countermanded, and the uncertain, hurried movements of the crew. She moved easily under full sail in the light breeze, heading for a berth conveniently close to the landing-place but right beneath a steep hill where the wind blew from all directions in fitful puffs; it was where he usually anchored; it was where everyone liked to anchor, and it was a bit congested. The yacht was put about whenever she could go no further on the tack she was on without regard to where the next tack would take her, and predictably overshot the only possible berth. It became urgently necessary to turn back downwind before she got in amongst the closely-packed small craft inshore, and she demonstrated her handiness by just making it despite her mizzen being pinned amidships, but it was a heart-stopping half minute which demoralized her crew. The anchor was let go on a dead run just as a fresh puff of wind took hold of her. Thanks to good preparation on the foredeck, the cable whizzed out cleanly, the anchor bit, and she snubbed dramatically round without touching anything. The yacht was at anchor, more or less in the intended position, and no material damage had been done, but what should have been an enjoyable and satisfying manoeuvre had turned out to be an alarming nightmare.

The owner in this story was clearly caught with his pants down when his entirely reliable engine became unavailable to him and exposed the inadequacy of his skill as a helmsman, but it was the decision to anchor in his usual berth where lack of space combined with an erratic wind to increase his problems (especially when it came to getting under way again) that revealed his shortcomings as a yachtmaster. For no matter how brilliantly a man may handle his vessel under sail or under power, he needs to be capable of sizing up a situation and making the right choice of objective, otherwise he will be continually relying on his dexterity to extricate himself from difficulties which he need never have got into.

The skipper's first concern is with aims. Whether in the planning or in the execution of a cruise he needs to have an aim firmly in view, to keep to it as long as it is relevant, to revise it or even scrap it and substitute another without hesitation if changing circumstances demand. The aim may be simple or complex; it may consist of several elements both long term and short term, but its priorities must be recognized. For example, the primary aim may be the winning of an offshore race, with the making of a particular landfall the immediate objective, when a rigging screw breaks. To press on at full speed would be to risk the mast and with it the attainment of the primary aim which must now be secured by the temporary introduction of a new aim to relieve the strain and effect repairs. In the same situation prolonged heavy weather might require the original aim to be superseded by that of preserving the strength of the crew or sea-room or both. Accident to a crew member or to a neighbouring competitor would almost certainly involve the substitution of a new aim.

The practical consideration of an aim in isolation from its attendant circumstances is impossible. Most of these circumstances are factors over which the skipper and crew have no control. Sometimes they are overriding, as for instance when a fixed period is available for the cruise, and then the aim has to be tailored to fit. More usually they present a mixture of handicaps and opportunities, to be circumvented or exploited through intelligence and ingenuity.

It is necessary to be on one's guard against ignoring a circumstance just because it ought not to be allowed to influence a decision. For instance it is generally accepted that shore-life considerations must not affect a seaman's judgement, but acceptance of this excellent principle confers no immunity from the powerful pressures involved, and the man who recognizes them is more likely to arrive at a sound decision than is he who writes them off as disqualified by the rules.

The most important element in a cruise is the crew. The statement of such an obvious fact seems superfluous, yet in all aspects of life we continually fall into the trap of subordinating the human interest to the material, of putting the needs of man's inventions above those of man himself. Yachtsmen can scarcely be blamed for erring in this respect; the deep bonds which have always grown between men and ships, the demand of good seamanship for meticulous maintenance, the spiritual deprivations of contemporary life, all combine to edge a man into the bizarre but not unusual situation of being owned by his property. The skipper to whom paint is more important than people is under a severe handicap; if he is uncertain of his ability as well the enthusiasm of his crew will soon evaporate.

The condition of the boat and her gear are of course extremely important and much thought and effort has to be devoted to the maintenance of a satisfactory standard, but it is skipper and crew who do this, or suffer the consequence of failure; it is them for whom the cruise is undertaken, they who carry it out, and their strength or weakness is the dominant influence on the outcome, exceeding that of either the weather or the boat.

In the planning stage the aim will be limited by the capability of the crew, or else the crew adjusted to match the demands of the aim. The adjustment does not necessarily entail any replacement of individual crew members; much can be achieved in a remarkably short time by training and practice, and most crews respond well to the stimulus of a training session.

The skipper in one boat may be the only competent seaman aboard, in another every member of the crew might be a competent skipper. The first will have to coach his crew through every evolution, supervising their every action, while the second hardly has to do more than indicate an intention, but each of them has his problems, each has a distinct role to play in eliciting the required performance.

If a man is to give a good account of himself he needs to know not only what to do and how to do it but why it is to be done. The performance of many crews falls far short of their potential because the skipper is overworked and the rest of the crew under-used, particularly in the matter of responsibility. A man who understands the skipper's intention works better and with more satisfaction than one who blindly obeys the current order; if he has been given responsibility as well he will be more conscientious.

An overtired skipper is a serious weakness in any crew. Fatigue makes a man irritable, impairs his judgement, saps his resolution and renders him prone to errors in calculation. The skipper's obligation to ensure that every one of his crew remains fit to do his job extends just as much to himself as to the others, and sensible delegation of work and responsibility is a simple and effective means to this end. It is a good plan to give everyone, according to his ability, the responsibility for some part of the ship or some aspect of the organization, thus bringing him into close personal involvement, strengthening the crew's sense of interdependence and relieving the skipper of many minor claims upon his attention and time. The spreading of navigational responsibility is a particularly valuable exercise in these respects and is incidentally the best way of eliminating the navigator's perennial moan that essential data has been inadequately recorded. It is important to match the task to the capacity of the individual so that those with talents have enough scope to exercise them and the less able can manage without obvious supervision.

When apportioning these duties among the crew, think first and hardest about the least gifted or experienced, identify the strong point of each so that it can be related to the service of the ship, and make these appointments early in the proceedings. Nothing undermines the shaky foundations of a rabbit's confidence so much as standing in the spotlight of a skipper's baffled gaze, after all the plum jobs have been dished out, while he racks his brains for something the halfwit can be trusted with. The best skippers, like the best theatrical directors, get unexpectedly good performances from their small-part players. They do this by convincing them of the value of their contribution, by bolstering up their confidence, and by giving generously and patiently of their own knowledge and experience. The next concern should be for the women in the crew. Too often it is automatically assumed that they will discharge all the domestic duties, thereby continuing, if they are wives and mothers, to work on holiday at their normal tasks but under conditions which are more difficult, frequently unpleasant and occasionally dangerous, while their menfolk enjoy a complete change from their normal occupations and disport themselves in the mentally and physically stimulating role of Conquerors of the Elements. Women make every bit as good helmsmen, deckhands and navigators as do men, and if a man cannot tidy a cabin, cook or wash up, a little practice will be a refreshing change from the office and will increase his value as a member of the crew.

The need for communication between skipper and crew is fundamental to their relationship. The skipper needs to be able to express his intentions and requirements, to teach, to give orders and to arrange for the feedback of information. The language will most probably be informal and the orders given in the form of requests, but there should be no ambiguity or uncertainty, and the recipients of an order should be perfectly clear about what is to be done, who is to do it and when. Habitual modes of speech are riddled with imprecision and it is necessary to be on one's guard if misunderstandings are to be avoided. The instruction to a helmsman 'Don't go too close to the breakwater' is a waste of breath because if the helmsman knows how close he can go without being 'too close' he hardly needs telling, and if he does not know and is not told, the only way he will find out is by disobeying. The words 'Steer for that buoy' will no doubt provoke grins in anticipation of the ensuing loud clang, the cloud of red dust and the skipper erupting through the hatch, but on at least one occasion when it really happened the collision was not caused by crassness on the part of the young girl at the helm, but by her total unpreparedness for the effect of the strong following stream, something the skipper could have eliminated by a more thoughtful instruction.

As well as uttering such incidental orders, a skipper will have to produce standing orders and lay down drills for specific operations. The purpose of standing orders is to safeguard the achievement of the aim; they do it in the main by reducing the risk of accident. Typical standing orders are prohibition of naked lights while filling petrol tanks, and requiring safety-harnesses to be worn in specified circumstances. The trouble with rules is that they have a built-in tendency to be self-defeating which increases with their number and complexity, as though there was only a fixed quantity of authority available to be spread over the words used. The wise man has the fewest possible rules and keeps them simple, avoiding all qualifying and conditional clauses. Drills are orders which detail the procedures to be followed in certain operations; they are designed to ensure that all essential actions are carried out in the correct sequence, and they incorporate a memorable pattern of action which is a powerful antidote to the paralysing effect of shock. Being based on action they can be permanently memorized by physical practice and thus escape the danger attendant on verbal orders of becoming swamped by their own numbers. The number and scope of drills can vary widely to suit the size and experience of the crew, the type of vessel and the operational circumstances, from an irreducible minimum of emergency drills such as Fire, Man overboard, Abandoning ship, to the coverage of routine operations like tacking and gybing. Great care needs to be taken over the content of drills to ensure that they are effective under all circumstances and do not incorporate variations to take account for instance of whether it is day or night, or whether one person rather than another has fallen in. If this is not done, different interpretations of the situation can result in dangerous confusion and doubt about which drill is to be applied. Drills can be sketched on paper but their design can only be perfected by practical experiment, and crews can only learn them by physical rehearsal.

In accepting the authority of the skipper the crew evinces discipline which, for practical purposes in the context of yacht cruising, means self-discipline. Essential to crew and skipper alike, it is the quality that enables people to live together in a confined space, to do a job properly under difficult, unpleasant and sometimes dangerous conditions, to choose the hard option, to act when they would rather wait and see, and to check when they would prefer to hope for the best. The most potent stimulus to self-discipline is example, and the skipper's prime concern will be to cultivate his own, setting a high standard and maintaining it come what may. It is when conditions are bad and attrition from cold, fatigue, seasickness and fear at their worst that the most conscientious performance is needed but the inclination to produce it is feeblest. At such a time it is useless trying to kick a performance out of a man who has given up, but if the atmosphere on board is one in which the maintenance of a proper standard is assumed as a matter of course, and the skipper leads from in front, the crew achieve a cohesion that gives great mutual support. This atmosphere, the product of overall crew morale, cannot be whipped up to order; it must be built up patiently from small elements, but once established it is an exceedingly strong structure.

The remaining area of a skipper's concern is with material things, the yacht and her equipment. To ensure that she is suitable for her purpose and to maintain her in a seaworthy state calls for a wide range of technical knowledge. This knowledge being easily accessible through books and the advice of specialists can be accumulated without great difficulty over a period of time through natural interest, and as long as the sources are readily available the inevitable gaps will cause a man less concern than the realistic appraisal of the extent and limitations of what he knows. In order to get the best out of a boat in the pursuit of his aim (and there are times when it is vital to get the best she can give), he needs a thorough understanding of her behaviour. The only way to arrive at this is by experiment, by handling her under the widest possible range of conditions and studying the effects of different techniques. There are no hard and fast rules governing the behaviour of every conceivable design of boat. Books and experts can explain why things happen, reveal the principles of cause and effect, suggest lines of enquiry, and in doing this are extremely valuable, but to expect more from them is rather like expecting to be able to make a passage because you have bought the charts.

PART I
SEAMANSHIP

I

LIVING AFLOAT

The seaworthiness of a vessel depends ultimately on the ability of her crew to maintain and handle her. To do this it is not enough that they should know what to do and how; they must be physically and mentally fit for action. A yacht of impeccable design and construction, faultlessly equipped and maintained, manned by a crew of experts, may yet come to grief if tools and equipment cannot be found when they are needed, if the crew is exhausted, helplessly seasick, or at loggerheads with one another. The art of seamanship begins with the ability of a crew to organize its life afloat in such a way that it can operate as a harmonious and efficient team under all circumstances, and the art of captaincy begins with the skipper's ability to provide the leadership and organization that will foster the development of an able, relaxed and happy crew.

Before we rush to produce a blueprint for crew efficiency the man on the foredeck, with the sea swirling up the legs of his oilskins, has a question. 'Why', he demands, spitting the bitter brine, 'am I here?' The answer is hardly thunderous but it is insistent and is endorsed by his habit of coming back for more. 'Because you are enjoying yourself mightily.' It is all too easy to allow an aim to slip out of sight in the enthusiasm of invention, and allow the production of ideas and the devising of means to obscure the ends which they are intended to achieve. The cold, wet, queasy, tired and fearful man on the foredeck will be back again and again because he finds what he came for; but despite the fact that a large measure of his satisfaction comes from participating in the work of a disciplined team, he will not come back if his every action is prescribed, every moment scheduled; the point of the exercise will have been lost.

Life afloat is dominated, in inverse proportion to the size of the vessel, by three factors. Space, which is limited to the size of the boat; motion, which is always present and can be violent; and water which in unlimited quantity is always in close proximity. Success is achieved by using the space intelligently, minimizing the effects of motion, and taking precautions against the invasive nature of water.

The limitation of space presents a problem that is partly a matter of stowage and partly a question of human relationships. Its solution is an interesting exercise in the assessment of priorities. A houseboat may be organized exclusively to provide the best in comfort and well-being for her crew but will never be fit to go to sea, while an ocean racer may be fitted out with every race-winning gadget and still be unfit to be at sea for more than a day or two unless the needs of her crew have been properly provided for.

Each member of the crew should have his own stowage space for personal gear, and every effort should be made to avoid his having to share this space with ship's equipment. Exclusive personal stowage is the best encouragement to the development of tidy habits which are essential for the avoidance of chaos when motion and water begin to make themselves felt.

In an ideal yacht all ship's gear would be stowed according to a logical plan, but in practice each item competes for space with its varying claims on security, accessibility, protection from weather and so on, and the final pattern is a compromise in which little trace of system may be evident. All the work of planning and contriving stowages will be wasted unless the crew know them and use them properly. This involves the complete acceptance by all of the principle that no job is finished until every tool and piece of gear has been returned to its stowage. Until everyone is reliable in this respect the skipper must be vigilant to detect and remedy lapses. Lessons may be learnt more quickly if, rather than taking the offender to task with oaths and rebukes, the skipper simply asks for the item concerned. The principle of returning objects to their correct stowage must be applied no less meticulously to navigational and galley equipment, and indeed to personal possessions as well. The navigator is entitled to put his hand on a chart, instrument or book where he expects to find it, and it is particularly infuriating for the cook, who has the hardest job in the boat, to have to search for a simple object like a serving-spoon which has been misplaced; his humour will not be improved if the proper spoon stowage contains a pair of spectacles, a packet of cigarettes or an odd glove.

The planning of stowages will naturally have taken account of the idiosyncrasies of the magnetic compass. Lapses of stowage discipline will sooner or later result in a discrepancy between the known deviation and that experienced by the compass. The danger is not the light-meter or beer can left on deck where it can be seen, but the thing parked behind an adjacent bulkhead or—worse—tucked into a wrong locker.

Most people have enough commonsense, imagination and forbearance to adapt to the confined living space of a small yacht without much strain or friction. At sea, the order imposed by a watchkeeping routine helps to smooth the progress of daily life. In harbour the skipper is more likely to have to influence events in order to prevent a free-for-all situation from developing. The character who insists on shutting himself in the heads for twenty minutes immediately after breakfast while he shaves and anoints himself 'because the cook has hot water on the go for washing up' may be deflected into the cockpit for his ablutions, or the hot water may be withheld until he has done the washing up.

A landsman, going aboard a properly fitted yacht for the first time, cannot fail to be impressed by the evidence with which she surrounds him that life at sea is dominated by motion. Everywhere fiddles and gimbals, arrangements of shock cord and lashings, wedges and turnbuttons, drawers that he cannot open until he has been shown the trick, remind him that at sea an object can and will move unless prevented. He may notice a chafed arc on a bulkhead where something has been left hanging, and if he comments on this he will almost certainly be told of clothes worn out without having been worn, destroyed by chafe in a hanging locker. He will also know about seasickness, expecting no doubt to suffer himself though hoping that commonsense precautions may afford some protection, and that if the worst befalls he will at least get it over tidily and unobtrusively. He will be very surprised to learn that motion has more subtle and insidious effects on the human frame than the blatant miseries of seasickness.

On a purely mechanical level the constantly reversing accelerations experienced by a boat in a seaway make every action more difficult; tasks take longer to perform and more effort has to be expended; the difference being quite disproportionate if the operator has to hold himself in position as well. Good design will ensure that a stable sitting position can be adopted for all essential tasks.

The effects on the brain are less easily counteracted. The symptoms, which vary with individuals and can affect even those who seldom reach the stage of vomiting, include blurring of the senses, buzzing in the ears and difficulty in focusing; impairment of co-ordination with resulting clumsiness of movement; slowing down of ratiocination to the point where calculation becomes laborious and prone to inaccuracy; and a strong disinclination to take as much trouble as one ought. The result is a lowering of performance and, more significantly, of standards so that jobs are done sloppily or postponed, and where strict reason would say 'This needs to be done better than would be necessary in fine weather. Let's do it properly now before things get worse'—the motion-sick mind says 'That'll do for now, we can tidy it up when things get easier'. Many deck logs that are scrupulously kept in fine weather when omissions are easily rectified, become so scanty as to be almost useless (and quite inadequate to trace the source of a plotting error) when things begin to get rough and accurate navigation becomes more important and more difficult.

The skipper can tackle this problem on two fronts. By simplifying the operations he can reduce the demands on his crew, and by cultivating his crew's morale he can help them to meet these demands. Any operation can be simplified by doing it in fine weather and all routine tasks ought to be cleared up when conditions are favourable, while a little anticipation will similarly dispose of others, but some things have to be done under all conditions of wind and weather and some only when things are tough. These should be studied to see how they can be improved, if need be by changing both methods and equipment, for we accept all manner of things as a matter of course because they are 'normal' without questioning their suitability to a particular boat and her crew. The aim of this exercise, which is to reduce the demands on the crew while maintaining the standard, needs to be kept firmly in mind.

This aim is a vital factor in relation to morale, because a very delicate balance has to be struck between overdriving a man and under-using him. Set an impossible or unreasonably high standard and your man will despair or lose faith in your judgement. Give the impression you care little how well the job is done and you rob him of all satisfaction save that of being able to knock off when it is finished. In dealing with the morale-sapping effects of motion-sickness the skipper is figuratively as well as literally in the same boat as his crew and is likely to suffer in the same way; he can help them best by anticipating the problem and being on his guard, by setting himself sensible standards and sticking to them.

Shore-based man out for an afternoon's sail can get wet and cold with impunity because of the hot bath, dry clothes and all the other blessings of the land that await him. Cruising man may have to remain wet and cold for a long time. A skipper needs to be able to educate and supervise novice crews who may be totally unprepared for the effects of wind-chill and the penetrative power of heavy spray. A cold man soon becomes depressed and sluggish, and his susceptibility to seasickness is increased. As a result he tends to put off going below for more clothes, gets still colder, and soon becomes incapable of making the effort. At this point he is beginning to suffer from exposure, a condition in which he needs help and must be regarded as a casualty. A healthy, well-nourished man feels cold if he is not wearing warm enough clothing, lacks a windproof outer garment, or if his clothes get wet, so everyone should be amply clad before going on deck and should don oilskins *before* water begins to come aboard. The skipper may detect signs of cold before a person will admit it to himself, and he should encourage the sufferer to do something about it immediately. He will also be able to anticipate the need for oilskins occasioned by a change of course, deteriorating weather or approach to rougher water, and give a lead to less experienced members of his crew.

Getting avoidably and unnecessarily wet is a crime against one's shipmates. Not only is a wet man less effective than a dry one, but his wet clothes (which cannot be dried until the salt has been rinsed out) become an unpleasant nuisance.

It has to be remembered that the effects of one's own crew's life extend to others. At sea, use some imagination about where and when garbage is jettisoned, and enforce an absolute veto on the dumping of any kind of plastic material. In harbour, forbid the dumping of refuse and see that it is either disposed of ashore in bin or bonfire, or take it out to sea. In appropriate areas, good gash habits can be engendered if all combustible waste including plastic is collected in a separate container and subsequently burned. Observe the decencies regarding noise in harbour, remembering that voices raised above the sound of an engine may be heard as raucous shouts by occupants of distant boats and local residents on shore. Even if it is calm, anticipate and silence that infernal tattoo from the halyards which will start as soon as the wind gets up.

When lying alongside other boats, instruct your crew in the manner of crossing their decks, avoiding the cockpit and main hatch, and keeping traffic to a reasonable minimum.

Going ashore in the dinghy, make it fast with ample scope away from the landing steps if possible. Sorting out a dinghy from a swarm is easy if the painters are long, exasperatingly difficult if they are clustered together on short scope like a bunch of grapes, and if the bunch is hard up against the landing steps it is almost impenetrable. Inflatables are supplied with painters that are too short, so if this defect remains uncorrected it can be made the occasion for a little instruction in splicing and whipping.

2

ROPEWORK

Ropes are a ship's sinews. Through them control is exercised and power is transmitted. Their proper use is the fundamental skill of the seaman on which depends the success of almost everything he undertakes. A rope smartly handled can save a life, bungled it can precipitate disaster. Careful planning, skilful helmsmanship and perfect co-operation can be brought to confusion and ruin by a single snarled line, and a skipper needs to be just as sure of his crew's ability to handle ropes as he is of the serviceability of the ropes themselves.

A rope's characteristics derive from the material of which it is made and the manner in which individual fibres are formed into the rope. The understanding of these characteristics is the most important factor in the correct use and handling of all kinds of ropes, and failure to take account of them is the usual reason why people get into a mess. The simplified review that follows is intended to illustrate the inherent natures of different kinds of rope in the cause of intelligent handling rather than to attempt a detailed description of all their properties.

Steel ropes

The great strength of steel is combined with the flexibility of fine wires to produce a rope of least thickness for a given strength. Such a rope has little stretch and offers little resistance to the wind so is well suited to use for standing rigging. Since each part is heavily loaded, apparently slight damage may cause severe weakening, and it is essential to avoid sharp bends and kinking. Greater flexibility, required for running rigging, is achieved by using a greater number of smaller wires in conjunction with a soft core; these fine wires are more vulnerable, especially when exposed to corrosion, but may easily and safely be spliced. Ropes that are formed of several strands (each strand being composed of a number of individual wires) can be bent round thimbles to form eyes, either by splicing or with the use of ferrules, because such ropes do not deform when so bent provided the radius is not too tight. The most commonly used standing rigging is, however, made from a small number or relatively thick wires forming a single strand (1 × 19); this cannot safely be bent into an eye because of the deformation which occurs, nor can it be spliced, so special terminal fittings have to be used. It is essential, when using any kind of terminal or ferrule, to fit exactly the right size and the correct material: aluminium ferrules on galvanized wire, copper on stainless. Abrasion is scarcely any problem with steel, but it should be remembered that the protective coating of zinc is easily removed from galvanized wire, especially in the smaller sizes. Stainless steel is particularly resentful of being bent, only a few reversals of a bend at one point being enough to cause fracture. Fortunately there is little occasion in the average boat to handle wire rope except when stripping or dressing the mast or renewing an item of rigging, so provided that coils are kept large and easy and care is taken to avoid kinking (most likely to happen when uncoiling), this material should not produce much of a problem.

Natural vegetable fibre ropes

Several kinds of vegetable fibre have been used in the past for making rope. At present their use in yachts is unusual because the greater durability and stability of the stronger synthetic fibres makes them worth the higher cost, but it is easy to imagine situations leading to a more widespread use of ropes made from plants rather than mineral products. The most striking characteristic of natural rope arises because the fibres absorb water. On becoming wet a rope gets thicker, shorter, stiffer and weaker than it was when dry. Dimensions of fairleads, cleats and the swallows of blocks have to allow for the increased diameter of wet rope.

Belays have to be finished off with a round turn to ensure that they can be cast off when wet (a half hitch can become immovable if put on dry and subsequently soaked). Halyards set up when wet slacken off and have to be sweated up again when they dry, and vice versa. In damp conditions vegetable fibres are liable to rot, so coils need frequent airing and should not be stowed in enclosed spaces when wet. Deterioration is easily detected by opening the lay and observing the state of the yarns on the inside of the strands; no matter how dirty or worn the outside of the rope, it is sound if the inside yarns are bright and fresh-looking and without visible ends; if the inside yarns are dull or discoloured and brittle with many ends, it is time to replace it. Before being put into service, new vegetable rope needs to be stretched otherwise it will develop kinks, resist attempts to coil it and become generally intractable. The method of stretching is to straighten out the length of rope, and having anchored one end, to put a strain on the other using a tackle if necessary. The strain is maintained for a few seconds so that the rope is evidently elongated, then relaxed completely and the rope allowed to lie on the ground. It will exhibit a tendency to twist (possibly actually rotating a turn or two) in a direction opposite to that of the lay. This should be encouraged by twisting the free end round and round as though to open the lay. The process of stretching and untwisting should be repeated until the elasticity of the rope is reduced and it no longer has any tendency to rotate when released. Large warps can be stretched by being towed astern while underway. Inferior though it undoubtedly is in all other respects, the best natural rope with its limited length of staple, subtle blend of pliability and elasticity, and high frictional properties is unbeatable as a material from which to make all the useful, protective and decorative knots, mats, sennits, eyes and coverings which practically furnished the world of the old-fashioned sailor, and in the creation of which he gained such an intimate understanding of the raw material and primary instrument of that world.

Synthetic ropes
Ropes made from manmade fibres are endowed with superior

strength, resistance to abrasion, and immunity from rot. They are un-affected by water and most oils and other substances likely to be encountered in the course of their use in yachts. If protected from chafe they have a remarkably long life and require very little maintenance, but most tend to harden with age, and some (notably those made from polyamides) deteriorate through exposure to ultra-violet light. Fortunately the extraordinary elasticity of polyamide (nylon) rope renders it more suitable for anchor and mooring warps which can easily be stored in the dark, than for running rigging which is necessarily exposed to daylight. Compared with vegetable ropes those made from synthetic fibres are slippery, especially when new, and even after wear has dulled the outside of a rope an extra turn is needed to winch-barrels, cleats and bollards, and an extra full tuck in splices. This slipperiness, combined with peculiarly inconvenient elastic properties which tend towards either total limpness or extreme springiness, make knots liable to undo themselves, particularly when intermittently loaded, so care is needed to see that suitable knots are used and that working ends are seized back to the standing part whenever necessary. These same characteristics virtually preclude the more exotic forms of knot-making which may involve unlaying the rope and reworking individual strands or yarns, consequently we never get on intimate terms with synthetic rope but always remain as it were at arm's length. A final property to be borne in mind is the low melting point of this type of rope, which allows cut ends to be fused quickly and easily to prevent unravelling, but raises the risk of serious accidental damage through frictional heating and contact with hot objects. When a rope's end is fused by heat it should also be given the protection of a sailmaker's whipping because the melted rope will eventually break up and unravel.

Construction of fibre rope

Vegetable fibres, being comparatively short, have to be locked together by being spun into threads, known as yarns, in order to produce continuity of strength over the length of the rope. The yarn is the smallest component of the rope to traverse its entire

length. Since synthetic fibres can be produced in continuous
filaments of any required length, a rope of adequate strength
could be made simply by gathering enough filaments into a parallel
bundle, but such a rope would be impossible to manipulate,
vulnerable, and weakened in practice through the unequal
sharing of load between the filaments. Organization of the fibres
is needed in order to impart qualities other than strength, and in
most yacht ropes the filaments are grouped into yarns which are
then either laid into the familiar spiral pattern or braided into con-
centric cylindrical sennits. In laid rope a number of yarns are
twisted together to form strands, and usually three strands are laid
up together into the final rope. In order to make the rope as strong
as possible it is necessary that the yarns should lie parallel to

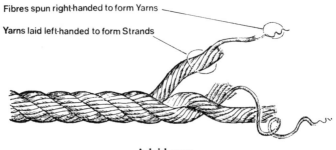

Fibres spun right-handed to form Yarns

Yarns laid left-handed to form Strands

A laid rope

the axis of the rope, so the direction in which the strands are laid
up together is opposite to that in which the yarns are twisted to
form the strands. This manner of twisting the components of a
rope in opposite directions reduces its tendency to unravel because
the torque produced by the yarns trying to untwist the strands
holds the strands more firmly into the lay, but it renders the rope
liable to form kinks which can jamb disastrously in sheaves and
fairleads. Where it is essential to eliminate the risk of kinking
even at the cost of reduced strength, as in lifeboat falls, the rope
is laid in the same direction as that in which the strands are twisted
to produce a special kink-resisting rope. The advantages of laid
rope are its resistance to abrasion, and the extreme ease with
which it can be spliced, thus allowing the formation of eyes and

the excision of local damage. Braided rope usually consists of a core of parallel yarns enclosed in one or more cylindrical braided sheaths. It is supple, kind to uncalloused hands, susceptible to chafe, difficult to form into eyes and virtually impossible to join by splicing, so severe local damage is apt to require the replacement of the whole rope.

Handling rope
Nearly all the troubles that arise in the handling of ropes stem from the formation of kinks, and nearly all kinks are the direct result of incorrect coiling. When a rope is coiled continuously in one direction, it is not only bent round in circles but is rotated on its axis, each rotation putting a turn in the rope. It is essential to start the coil at the fixed end and work towards the free end so

Coiling a rope, turns travelling to the free end

that the turns can escape off the end of the rope. If the coil is begun at the free end the turns cannot escape, they are imprisoned in the rope as a series of vindictive kinks. The direction of coiling is dictated by the lay of the rope. Nearly all rope is laid right-handed and must be coiled clockwise. Left-handed rope exists although it is unusual, so the direction of the lay should always be checked when handling a strange rope, if left-handed it has to be

27

coiled counter-clockwise. The consequence of coiling in the wrong direction is an instant snarl-up as soon as the rope straightens out from the coil, turns interlace, kinks blossom all over the landscape, picking up more turns, embracing them with half-hitches, and if a strain should come on it will take a long time to unravel the mess. Many a horrid tangle that is dumped into the arms of helpers when coming alongside, many a good rope that is maligned as 'Impossible' owe their state entirely to having been coiled in the wrong direction. Braided rope can be coiled in either direction, and if they are long it may be advisable to change the direction every hundred feet or so. To prevent figures of eight forming in the coil, it is necessary to impart a slight twist in the same direction as that required to open the lay. In braided rope the direction of this twist is related to the direction of coiling, but the knack is quickly acquired and after a little practice on laid rope, becomes automatic.

The size of the turns in a coil are kept even by reaching out and grasping exactly the same amount of rope with each movement of the working hand. The diameter of the coil should be related to the size and nature of the rope; if too small the coil will be inconveniently bulky, if too large it will be sloppy and difficult to keep in shape. It is, however, often a good idea to make up lines that are going to be stowed away in extra large coils which can then be twisted into sausages after being stopped with four pieces of marline. When untwisted again the coil will be found in good shape with less chance of the turns having got through one another than if the coil had been dumped straight in a locker. Coils that have been stored should always be coiled afresh before being put into use.

The thrown part of a heaving-line will fly better if it is wet and coiled small. Anchor and towing warps or any line that runs out horizontally should always be flaked rather than coiled when being prepared for use otherwise there is a risk of a turn being picked up out of its correct order and precipitating a foul-up could result in an accident or injury.

The falls of halyards are normally very much exposed and need to be well secured against the sea coming aboard when the weather gets bad or they will soon be trailing over the side. A good sea-gasket will hold the coil firmly in place and preserve its shape ready for immediate running; the type used should be made standard for the vessel and every member of the crew should be familiar with it, otherwise there will occur a variety of unseamanlike exhibitions ranging from the delayed lowering of a sail while a perfectly good halyard coil is transformed into a tangle to be interminably sorted out and re-coiled, to the dramatic ascent of the mast by the intact coil as soon as the belay is cast off. To prepare the fall of a halyard for running the turns of the sea-gasket must first be taken off and the coil laid right way up on deck. Right way up means with the running part on top, and the end coming out clear of the coil from the bottom. Some skippers will insist on always coiling or flaking the fall afresh before lowering, and this should invariably be done if there is the least doubt about the fitness of the coil to run, but if the coil was well made in the first place, properly secured and carefully prepared there will be no reason for qualms.

The whole point about rope is that you toil at one end of it and the ardently desired result of your labours occurs at the other end. Or so you hope. If it does not it is ten to one something extremely regrettable is happening and the harder you pull the more you will be sorry when you find out what it is. It is very easy for a man to become engrossed in what he is doing at his end of a rope and to forget that it is what is going on at the other end that matters, and a skipper who fails to educate his crew in this respect invites unwelcome dramas and avoidable damage.

3
DECKWORK

'You make it look so easy, but then you know what you are doing.' We have all been sparked into similar comment by the performance of an expert, and a well trained and well led crew give the impression that they have an easy time as they go about their tasks without haste or apparent exertion, and most conspicuously without noise. By contrast, an incompetent crew presents a scene of frenzied activity, hurtling round the deck to the accompaniment of a pandemonium of shouting. Onlookers rightly conclude that since they make it all look so difficult they cannot know what they are doing, perhaps not even what they are supposed to be doing. The skipper would have to be insane if he felt jauntily confident of having the situation entirely under control.

It would be tedious, besides making this book far too long, to discuss the skipper's approach to every aspect of deckwork, so it is proposed to take a series of typical operations such as might be encountered in the course of a day's sail and use them to illustrate this approach.

Weighing anchor
This operation is part of the evolution of 'getting under way' which has as its object the transfer of control of the vessel from her anchor to the helmsman. The skipper will have decided his route out of the anchorage, the sails he will carry and the sequence in which they are to be set, in the light of the situation presented by the surroundings, the way the yacht is lying under the influence of wind and tide, the strength and direction of the wind, the ability of her crew and the performance of the boat.

The critical part of the operation is the period between the breaking of the anchor's grip of the bottom and its emergence above the surface of the water, during which time the yacht's response to control is hampered by the length of cable and the anchor hanging from her stem. The duration of this critical period will depend on the depth of water and the speed with which the anchor can be brought to the surface. Assuming that there is no tidal stream and therefore no steerage way while the boat is still anchored, and that it is necessary to get away on a particular tack, the timing of the breaking out of the anchor is crucial to success. Let us imagine first what is likely to happen if an inexperienced crew is given no other instruction beyond 'Right, boys, get it up'. The boys throw themselves energetically into the task of shortening in the cable. The work gets heavier and they begin to tire. When it is up and down there is a minute or so of back-breaking struggle while the mud is persuaded to relax its grip (the skipper meanwhile anxiously wondering what the hell), and then they wearily lug cable and anchor foot by foot to the surface. If the yacht has paid off on the right tack it will have been by pure chance, though a strong crew in a light boat sometimes succeed undeservedly through their energy imparting steerage way to the boat.

In order to eliminate the uncertainty from this operation the crew need to understand the skipper's intention, the part they have to play in it and the information that must pass between them. As the vital factor in this instance is the timing of the breaking out of the anchor, the skipper needs to be kept informed of the progress of shortening in, a foredeck hand reporting the cable marks as they appear on deck. The skipper may decide to shorten in to a particular mark, or if the holding is good and the anchor well dug in, to continue until the cable is up and down. He will tell the foredeck party of his decision, warn them to shorten in steadily and conserve their energy for a quick break out and recovery of the anchor which will be timed to synchronise with the commencement of a yaw on to the required tack. He is also likely to want to know the direction in which the cable is growing, the moment when the anchor breaks out, and when it is finally clear of the water. Once a crew has become proficient it suffices to tell them on which tack it is intended to get away and they will be able to judge the timing correctly, but the skipper should still make sure that he is kept in touch with the progress of the operation.

The routine of weighing is completed by the secure stowage of the anchor, its cable or warp and any tools used such as windlass levers, and any action needed to exclude water from the navelpipe.

Stowage of anchor
An anchor is a heavy object offering considerable resistance to moving water and if its stowage for seagoing is insecure it may break loose and cause great damage. Security depends on both the design of the stowage arrangement and its correct use. A set of deck chocks may be strong enough but if the lashing that holds the anchor into them lets go or stretches because it was put on wrongly they cannot do their work. The outboard stowage of anchors exposes them to severe strains in heavy weather and many skippers will insist on stowing them inboard when going offshore, but coastal waters can deliver hard knocks and all fittings and fastenings should be examined carefully and frequently to check that they are up to the job and not showing signs of distortion or movement. Particularly suspect are removable pins which exercise direct as opposed to indirect restraint. An example of direct restraint is a pin which passes through a fairlead and holds an anchor in position. Indirect restraint is exemplified by a pin which prevents the opening of a hinged catch so designed as to hold an anchor without transmitting load onto the pin. In the former case overloading the pin can distort it and prevent its withdrawal. In the latter the function of the pin is the same as if it were used with a hasp and staple, it locates the load-bearing members without itself taking any load.

Making and handing sail
The successful completion of an evolution in harbour is no guarantee that the same people, using the same methods, will

Erupting from a Highland loch in a mountain squall is the author's 47ft yawl, *Ismana*. Designed by J. Laurent Giles, she was a notable competitor in RORC Class 2 during the 1950s under her former name, *Cheemaun* (*David Burnett*)

Owl, a 55ft ketch designed by F. Shepherd and built in 1900, close-hauled in the North Minch. Photographed from the author's 31ft cutter, *Varangian* (*John Russell*)

succeed at sea, but anything which has worked satisfactorily at sea will be equally effective in sheltered water. If a technique that has been devised, tested, perfected at sea is adopted as standard procedure under all circumstances the crew reap the reward of much valuable practice. The advantages of this course are not equal for all operations and it should not be followed blindly, but where sail handling is concerned the exercise should always be considered in its seagoing context.

The order to bend on and hoist no. 1 jib invites a series of questions which if the organization is right will be answered without their having been asked. The first is 'Which is no. 1 jib and where is it kept?' The answer is given by having a uniform system of marking both sails and bags, ensuring that sails are stowed always in their own bags, and that there is evident logic in the organization of the sail locker. The next question, which arises when the sailbag has been lugged up on deck, is 'How am I going to get this little lot hoisted the right way up and with no twists in it?' If the answer can only be found by spreading the sail out on deck, identifying the tack and starting to clip on the hanks from there, the yacht cannot claim to be fit for sea. If the sail has been bagged in a suitable manner it can be bent on under close control without any risk of a snarl-up or of hoisting it up-side-down, and there is a simple single-handed method which allows the sail to be bent on entirely within the bag, and hoisted straight out of it. The key to this operation lies in the sail being bagged while still hanked to the stay; additional precautions which have to be taken are soon revealed by experiment.

Getting a sail bent on without mistakes is just a question of forethought. Real difficulty comes when the halyard is attached, especially in the dark, because several nasty things can happen which can be quite difficult to straighten out. The least of these is getting a turn of the halyard round the forestay; it may be brought about either by passing the halyard round the stay, or by bringing the head of the sail up round the stay when clip-ping on the halyard. In daylight it can be avoided by looking aloft when bending on, but at night it may not be possible to see well enough and you may end up with more turns than one through groping attempts to sort things out. The only sure solution is to adopt a standard procedure for shifting the end of the jib halyard from the sail being handed onto its attachment point on the pulpit or wherever, and back to the head of the next sail to be set, along a set path that never varies. More serious problems arise if a bight of the halyard gets round a spreader, and in a rough sea it can become elaborately entwined. Apart from the difficulty of disentangling it from the deck, there is the danger that if it is not noticed, the hand on the halyard, feeling resistance, may use the winch and break something. If he is a good hand, and you have trained him properly, he will know what is happening at the other end of his rope and will stop in time, but on a dark night with heavy spray battering at him . . . The only certain safeguard is to make sure there is never any excess slack in the halyard, remembering that it can easily be introduced by the head of the sail creeping up the stay. Two people can cope if they take enough trouble, but a single-hander may have to stop down the head of the sail with stuff that will break when the sail is hoisted. Although the sail under discussion is a headsail, all halyards need watching for excessive slack.

When the time has come to hoist a sail it should go up smartly, the luff should be tightened and the sheet trimmed with the least possible delay. A half-set sail is a handicap, an obstacle to manoeuvrability, and if it is flogging, a menace to itself and to anyone within reach of its flailing sheets. The operation is completed by coiling down and securing the fall of the halyard, and returning the winch handle and the sailbag to their stowage.

A taut luff is essential to the proper setting of a sail. Not only will the sail decline to take up an efficient aerodynamic shape if the luff is slack, but damage may be caused by the unfair strains imposed. With headsails the condition is so obvious that it is usually soon noticed and rectified, but judging by the number of times mainsails are seen with slack luffs, their boom-ends dragged harshly down into cockpits (a sight to make one wince), it would seem that the condition is often incorrectly diagnosed and the mainsheet given an extra pull in an attempt to improve the poor set of the sail.

Misuse of the topping-lift is a possible reason for failure to achieve a taut luff, along with some other difficulties in handling mainsails. In the smaller yachts where the weight of the boom is insignificant, the full function of the topping-lift may not be appreciated and perfectly adequate results may be attained by treating it merely as a preventer to stop the boom falling on the deck when the sail is lowered. But with a heavier boom and longer luff it will be found that unless the boom is raised so that the angle it makes with the mast is smaller than the angle between the luff and foot of the sail, its weight will transmit a diagonal strain through the sail onto the luff slides and track. The resulting friction will act as a brake on the slides and may be powerful enough not only to stop the mainsail from coming down when the halyard is slacked off, but to require considerable exertion in dragging it down. For the same reason hoisting is made harder work and the final tension on the luff may not be reached. When

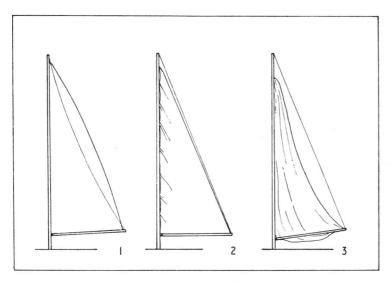

The topping lift: use and misuse; (1) luff set up taut. Topping lift slack enough to allow the sail to set close-hauled. Hardly any strain on the luff slides; (2) slacking the halyard without setting up the topping lift transfers the strain on to the luff slides. Sail will not come down; (3) topping lift set up, halyard slack. Sail coming down easily.

this kind of difficulty is experienced it is worth trying the effect of topping up the boom a bit more before worrying about lubricating the slides or looking for loose track screws, though the latter may well be discovered because sailing with a slack luff exposes the mast track to loads which it should not be asked to endure.

The tension on the foot of a boomed sail is easily adjusted to suit the wind strength and the cut of the sail, the right amount being quickly discovered by experiment.

Setting and sheeting of sails affords the most usual occasion for the appearance of riding turns on winches. If these occur regularly it is probably a sign that the lead of the sheet to the winch needs altering but they are also sometimes introduced by a hand giving a 'helpful' heave ahead of the winch. A riding turn on a sheet winch is easily cleared and the exercise can be useful crew training, but if one should occur on a halyard winch during the final stages of sail hoisting and the sail is winched up tight, there may be no way of relieving the strain and clearing it except by cutting the shackle at the tack. Instruction in the use of winches is a necessary part of every crewman's education if injury and damage is to be avoided, and the subject of riding turns can be covered at the same time.

Handing sail is a potentially trickier job than hoisting. This is partly because the sail is under less firm control when being lowered, and partly because the reason for handing the sail is often an increase in the wind to the point where it can no longer be carried. The difficulties are minimized by careful preparation and crew briefing, and by thoughtful handling of the yacht. Preliminaries consist of deciding how many hands are needed for the job, appointing each to his specific task, and seeing that he has the necessary equipment, gaskets, sailbag and so on. It is better to have too few than too many at the start because it is easier to send in reinforcements than to withdraw superfluous troops, and too many people get in each other's way. If not racing, the handling of the yacht should be aimed at making things easy for the deck party. Depending on the individual boat and the weather, deck work is easiest when running before the wind, and a large headsail comes down in a very docile manner if it is lowered

when collapsed in the lee of the mainsail. If running is imprac-
ticable, or if lowering a mainsail, the next best plan is to sail close-
hauled, pinching to get the speed as low as possible while still
retaining full control; this eases the motion and reduces the
amount of water coming over the foredeck, but in anything of
a breeze a headsail will not come down unless it is pulled. The
most difficult conditions are produced by the helmsman ramping
full to windward. The priorities when handing a sail are to eliminate unwanted slack in the halyard, to ensure that the sail comes
down on deck, not into the sea, and to bring it quickly under
control. As soon as the sail is lowered the end of the halyard
needs to be secured so that the fall can be pulled tight and
belayed. Only after this has been done is the halyard hand free to
secure and stow the sail. The reason for not letting the sail go over
the side is sometimes not understood by novice crews who may
think it is to do with not getting the sail wet. They should be
instructed that if a large jib goes in the sea its recovery should be
begun from the forward end, each section being secured as it is
brought aboard, and warned that an attempt to bring the clew
aboard first may result in their being dragged overboard.

Recovering the jib: the difficult way

Recovering the jib: the easy way

One of the lessons that is brought forcibly home by the experience of heavy weather is that sails need to be carefully and securely stowed. If this is not done, wind and sea will soon work them loose and someone has to go and do the job again, probably under conditions which have become more unpleasant and maybe dangerous. Gaskets should be abundant and of ample strength for seagoing conditions.

Reefing

Besides increasing the strains on rig and hull, strong winds stretch sailcloth into fuller curves and increase heel angle, redistributing the aerodynamic and hydrodynamic forces to augment weather helm. By the simple expedient of furling the lower, and most accessible part of a triangular sail, the act of reefing has the effect of removing a strip from the leech, reducing the area and bringing it lower and further forward. Slab reefing confers the additional benefit of flattening the sail and so further reducing its luffing and heeling power. Despite its theoretical attractions

40

the operation is looked on as a chore to be avoided as much as possible, and most of us prefer to change headsails, wrestling with acres of wet canvas on exposed foredecks, rather than reef the mainsail. Part of the trouble is that all too often the simplicity and ingenuity of the idea is not matched by the methods and equipment used to carry it out.

Roller reefing is quick and economical of manpower, but it is virtually impossible at sea to apply any tension to the foot of the sail, the bulk of rolled luff causes distortion, and the boom is apt to droop, so the set of the sail tends to deteriorate the deeper it is reefed and this limits the depth of reef that can be taken.

Slab reefing is a rather more complicated operation which can be hard work for a single-hander. Carefully performed however, it can result in an excellently setting sail, deeply appreciated when clawing to windward in dirty weather.

Since shaking out an unwanted reef is such a simple matter, and reefing is done so much more easily and more comfortably at anchor, commonsense and seamanlike prudence conspire to limit the occasions on which reefs are taken at sea to genuine need. It is nevertheless important for a crew to practise reefing at sea so that the job can be done as efficiently and safely as it is in harbour.

The greatest difficulty is caused by the yacht's motion, and it is worth taking advantage of any opportunity that may exist of gaining even a partial lee in which to work. Failing this the yacht should be handled with the object of maintaining a steady and moderate angle of heel together with modest speed. Movement of the boom should as far as possible be eliminated. Even if the boom can swing only a few inches from side to side, the crew will spend more time and energy in clinging to it than they do in working; if it is sweeping a couple of feet there is little chance of their doing an even half decent job and a real risk that someone's grip may be broken and that he will be injured in a fall or thrown overboard. The ideal arrangement is to secure the spar in a strong gallows of convenient height for working, as this provides solid support and increases safety and speed. It is quite usual to find that provision for securing the luff pennant is inadequate. You can extemporize for the first reef by lashing the pennant round the gooseneck, but the second produces a horrid looking mess and the third is impossible. There are several ways of circumventing this defect, all of which need some previous preparation; one is to use a large bow shackle for the tack and to attach the reef cringle to this by a twisted shackle. It pays to be generous in slacking both the main halyard and clew outhaul. Moving to the leech of the sail, life will be easier for those who have previously rove the leech pennant but the bee-block is likely to have been positioned according to a rule-of-thumb established for gaff sails whose requirements are somewhat different; if so the lead of the pennant will pull the cringle vertically downward onto the boom instead of aft. Best results are obtained if the lead of the pennant is modified and a separate lashing used to reduce the drift between the cringle and the boom. If a batten has to be removed it is most easily and safely done after the cringle above it has been pulled down and secured, and the pocket is in the fold of 'dead' sail which is not affected by the flapping of the leech. When shaking out a reef replace the batten while the portion of the sail containing the pocket is still immobilized by the pennant. With the hauling down and securing of luff and leech cringles the reef is essentially complete. Rolling the fold of surplus sail and tying it above the boom by the reef points is a tidying up process having no effect on the set sail if the reef has been correctly taken. If, after the sail has been re-set and trimmed, V-shaped puckers appear at the reef points, local strain is indicated. If most are affected, it is a sign that the clew outhaul has not been slacked off enough or that the leech cringle has not been hauled far enough aft. Isolated puckers can be eliminated by slight easing of the corresponding reef points. In shaking out a reef the order of actions is exactly reversed. The appropriate reef points may be cast off while still sailing, and it is essential that none are omitted, then with the boom slightly topped up and the halyard a little slackened, first the leech and then the luff pennants are let go, and the sail is hoisted up and re-set.

The unpractised and inexperienced are prone to display some reluctance to reef if the wind freshens while they are underway, postponing the decision in the hope that the increase in the wind is only temporary. Eventually, heavily overpressed, they are forced to do it under worse conditions than if they had acted promptly. Familiarity with the exercise and the ability to interpret the development of weather are recommended antidotes.

Mooring alongside

When a vessel has been manoeuvred into her berth she needs to be secured so that neither wind, tide nor the action of other vessels can cause damage to her or her neighbours. Preparation for this operation consists in briefing the crew, rigging fenders to prevent direct contact between the yacht and her berth, a check rope to ensure that she is brought up in the berth, and mooring lines fore and aft to hold her in position while a permanent moor is made.

Crew briefing will explain the skipper's intention and the part played in it by each member of the crew; it will naturally include the approach to the berth and plans to cater for unexpected developments, matters not strictly part of the exercise under discussion and dealt with under the heading of 'Handling'. The nature of the berth and presence or absence of assistance on shore are likely to be determining factors in deciding for instance whether crew members need to be landed before the yacht can be secured, whether heaving lines will be needed, and so on. It will also be necessary to assess the probable behaviour of the yacht after she has lost way as this will dictate the priorities in mooring. Inexperienced crews will have to be taught the need to catch a turn with their lines round something solid while they still have enough slack to do it. No figure is more poised for instant comedy or tragedy (depending on the onlooker's involvement) than the one standing on deck or dockside holding in his hands a rope at the other end of which several tons of boat is in motion. No hitches or knots are necessary, a single round turn provides enough friction to give control and more can be added if the strain is exceptionally heavy, but it is no good waiting until all the slack has been taken up because by then the attempt may lead to injury as well as failure.

Fenders need to be well spaced out over the boat's length and rigged at heights which will give them most effect. If possible at least one fender should be kept in reserve, ready to be interposed wherever it may be needed. They are bulky objects, taking up a disproportionate amount of the available stowage space, but it has to be admitted that if a yacht's fenders do not present a stowage problem they are probably inadequate.

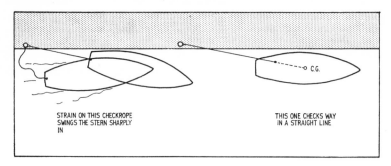

STRAIN ON THIS CHECKROPE
SWINGS THE STERN SHARPLY
IN

THIS ONE CHECKS WAY
IN A STRAIGHT LINE

C.G.

Using a check rope

If the check rope is led from the centre of the stern it will pull the stern sharply in the berth when the strain comes on and may cause damage. The ideal lead would be through the vessel's centre of gravity, which would enable her to be brought up without yawing either way, but this could be difficult to arrange if there is no suitably located strong point, and a reasonable compromise might be on the quarter if the stern is broad, or the strongest cockpit winch. When the shore end has been secured, the check rope should be surged carefully round a bollard or winch so as to take the way off gently and never snubbed. The check rope should invariably be rigged and ready for use even when it is intended to bring up by going astern on the engine because there are at least three likely reasons why a perfectly serviceable engine can fail to deliver power when put astern and no means of checking any of them before the actual event.

In most situations it will be desirable to secure the bow as soon as the way is off, to prevent it being swept round by wind or tide. If led from the stem the bow line will slant the bow in to the berth, and though eventually the aim will be to align the boat parallel, it can be helpful if she is held rather bows-in until all the mooring lines have been rigged. The check rope can usually be made to serve as a temporary stern line, if necessary adjusting the lead to a point nearer the stern. As soon as the yacht has settled the fenders should be checked and adjusted, and then the permanent moorings can be rigged.

The minimum mooring lines for a yacht are bow and stern lines and forward and after back springs; breast ropes can usually be dispensed with unless they are seen to be needed. Bow and stern lines should be long and well spread fore and aft, with ample allowance for the range of tide. If lying outside another boat they should be led to the shore. Springs do most of the work in keeping the boat in position and are the prime means of stopping her from surging about, displacing fenders and starting all kinds of mischief which can even extend to damaged spreaders and masts, but it is often a major problem when lying alongside another yacht to find a suitable point at which to make them fast. However, if one's own vessel is provided with a strong mooring cleat or bollard on each bow about 20 per cent of the LWL abaft the stem, and a similar one on each quarter, it is possible to make do even if the neighbour has only single mooring points on the centreline at bow and stern. These four mooring points at shoulders and quarters are immensely useful for all sorts of purposes. A boat will often lie more quietly in a strong stream if head and stern lines are attached to them, and they provide convenient leads for boom guys and similar temporary tackle.

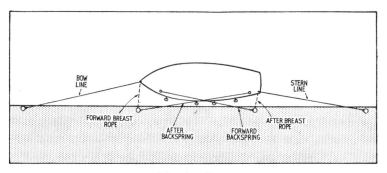

Mooring lines

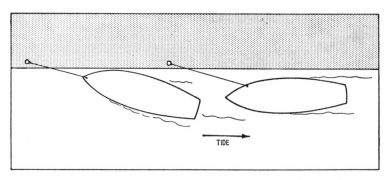

Lying alongside in a tideway: effect of shifting the lead of a mooring line

Anchoring

A yacht may anchor for a variety of reasons and in widely differing circumstances. She may anchor in shelter for a night or more during which her crew may go ashore for short periods and will for part of the time be sleeping. She may anchor temporarily for an hour or two during the day while the crew make a brief expedition ashore, swim, fish, eat or effect repairs. Occasionally she may kedge for the duration of a foul tide when becalmed, and a disabled vessel might have resort to her ground tackle to save her from drifting into danger. The purpose of anchoring will affect the choice of berth and the method and tackle used. Thus for a temporary anchorage on a rising tide, the berth chosen could be dry at low water and the tackle consist of a light kedge and line that would be easy to recover. For an overnight stay, questions of depth and swinging room, quality of holding, degree of shelter and the possibility of the wind freshening or changing direction while the crew are asleep would influence a skipper's decision to use his best bower anchor on a good scope of cable or even to moor with two anchors.

An anchor grips the sea-bed because it is so designed that a horizontal pull causes it to dig itself in, the harder the pull the deeper it digs. Changing the pull from horizontal to vertical converts the shank of the anchor into a lever which breaks the grip of the fluke and allows it to be lifted out of the ground. Secure holding depends on dropping the anchor onto material which is soft enough for it to dig in but stiff enough to resist further motion once it is buried. The best medium consists of finely divided particles such as clay, mud and sand of sufficient depth to allow the anchor to bury itself. Rock cannot be penetrated, and although an anchor may gain a hold in a crevice, this hold might equally be permanent or be broken suddenly and the anchor then slide without gaining another. Gravel, shingle,

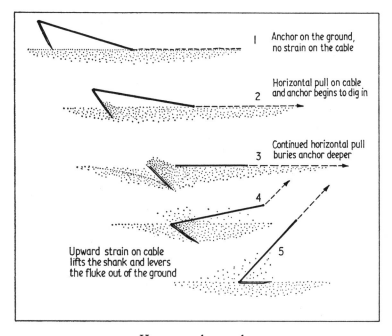

1   Anchor on the ground, no strain on the cable

2   Horizontal pull on cable and anchor begins to dig in

3   Continued horizontal pull buries anchor deeper

4

Upward strain on cable lifts the shank and levers the fluke out of the ground

5

How an anchor works

volcanic ash and very soft mud allow the anchor to dig in but lack the mechanical strength to hold it. Anything on the bottom that prevents the fluke of the anchor from penetrating will prevent it from getting a proper hold. Thus if the fluke lands on an old tin, bicycle wheel, doormat, coil of rope, bulky weed such as kelp, or part of the yacht's own anchor cable the anchor is liable to drag when a strain comes on it. The further an anchor travels over the ground before digging in the greater the probability that it will encounter some such object.

47

In order to ensure that the anchor will hold it is necessary not only that it should be dropped on good holding ground but that:

1   The anchor should arrive first, before any cable.
2   The cable should run unchecked so that the anchor is not moved prematurely.
3   The anchor is struck home by a firm horizontal pull on the cable.

The first of these requirements is easy to meet but it occasionally happens that a bight of cable is allowed to run out before the anchor is let go, and this should be guarded against. The free running of the cable is a matter of preparation, either by good stowage in the locker or by ranging enough cable on deck, and having the cable clearly marked at intervals of five fathoms or ten metres. The horizontal pull is obtained by refraining from snubbing the cable until enough scope has run out; the amount depends on the depth of water and the weight of cable, a heavy chain might need no more than three or four times the depth while a warp should have five or six times. It is best to have some way on while veering cable in order to ensure that the anchor is

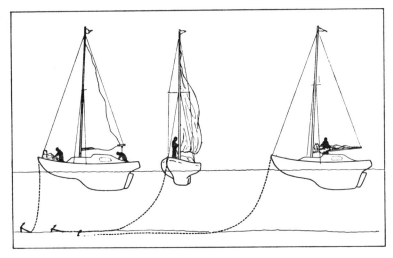

Anchoring

properly set in and that the yacht does not simply lie to the bight. This is essential if a fisherman-type anchor is used because otherwise cable may foul the anchor and trip it as soon as strain comes on. Patent anchors are supposed to be proof against this kind of fouling and even if the chain is dropped in a heap on top it will nearly always pull clear and the anchor bite successfully, but a foul-up can happen and it is in any case best to make sure that the anchor is holding by watching it take way off the boat and swing her round to it.

Where the bottom is foul with moorings or heavy rubbish a buoyed tripping-line will be needed. This should be long enough to reach the surface at highwater, strong enough to withstand the heavy strain that may be required to free a fouled anchor, and be made of a line that will not float and be a menace to anyone under power. The skipper delegates a man for the job telling him where it is intended to go, what commands and signals will be used, what tackle is to be used, how much cable is to be ranged or warp flaked on deck and at what mark it is to be snubbed. Parallel instructions will also be given to those responsible for handing sail and any other operations forming part of the evolution.

Further discussion at this point moves out of the province of deckwork into handling, but one factor vital to both is timing. Precise knowledge of how long to allow for the preparation and execution of an operation takes fine judgement and contributes as much to polished performance as does skilful helmsmanship. Haste is the enemy breeding mistakes and confusion. Speed grows by itself out of the experience of success. If ample time is allowed from the outset and the job done right, 'ample time' becomes a diminishing quantity.

Criticizing and adapting methods and gear, devising fresh techniques and equipment are an essential part of a skipper's approach to deckwork and seamanship generally. His criterion will be practicability, the test success in doing the job, the value of a piece of equipment the amount of work it does for him compared with how much he does for it.

4

THE DINGHY

No part of a yacht's equipment is called upon to perform so many different funtions as her tender. The dinghy may operate as ferry, workboat for laying out a kedge, running out warps or cleaning the topsides, as survey craft, rescue boat or bathing raft. In the course of her employment she may be lashed on deck, stowed in a locker, streamed astern, propped against a hedge or tethered to a quay. The tender's condition and the manner in which she is handled accurately reflect the standards which prevail on board the parent vessel, and as good a way as any of assessing the competence of the members of an unknown crew joining a yacht for the first time is to watch them ferrying themselves and their gear aboard in a dinghy.

As long as the same principles of commonsense and sound seamanship are applied to the management of the dinghy as to the parent vessel no problems need arise and it would seem that a skipper need devote no more attention to the subject than to any other important part of the yacht's equipment. Yet accidents happen and lives are lost in the operation of dinghies even in sheltered water, so it is sensible to seek reasons why and in what respect lapses of accepted standards occur.

The trouble lies principally in the less 'serious' uses to which the dinghy is put, as liberty boat or just for messing around in harbour when we tend to be off guard, become careless or are tempted to take short cuts by overloading to save an extra journey. Some of the dinghy work in harbours also involves visitors to the yacht who may lack previous boating experience.

When a dinghy is being used for a task like laying out a kedge which clearly calls for care and good seamanship one would

Varangian, built for the author in 1960 by James Smith of Lerwick, encourages long passages because she was designed for living at sea (*David Burnett*)

Blue Charm, designed by Illingworth and Primrose in 1959, had a remarkable light airs performance probably as a result of the laminar flow achieved over her underbody (*Alan Hollingsworth*)

expect someone competent to be in charge and the whole operation to be under the control of the skipper or an experienced mate.
It is equally important for a competent person to be in charge
when the dinghy is making a ferry trip to or from the shore, and
everyone involved should know who that is. To be competent
means not only proficient in handling the boat but knowing the
maximum load, its correct distribution, and being able to anticipate and prevent dangerous actions by the uninstructed.

An inflatable dinghy propelled by oars is to some extent
protected against overloading because it becomes almost impossible to row when deep-laden. With too many people in the
boat the oarsman has too little room to work and cannot get his
blades clear of the water. An outboard motor, however, will drive
an overloaded boat which is by definition in danger of swamping
and is in potential peril because the oars cannot be used if the
engine fails.

In any type of dingy the loss or breakage of an oar can be the
first link in a chain of events that leads to disaster, so all hands
should be scrupulously careful in the handling of oars which
should never be thrown about or used as levers. In this context
the ability to scull with a single oar may be vital and it is sensible
to ensure that a rigid dinghy has a sculling notch. An inflatable
with its lack of determination to go where it is pointing can be
sculled broadside in quiet weather, though the want of a whole
pair of oars would make it helpless in a strong breeze.

If the crew of a dinghy find themselves in the water their lives
may depend on their being able to hold on to her. Inflatables have
grab lines, wooden dinghies may be fitted with grab rails on the
bilges, but some glass fibre dinghies present no handhold of any
kind and this defect needs to be rectified before a dinghy can be
considered fit for service.

The launching, manning and recovery of a dinghy while
underway is not a frequent operation, but as it might have to be
done with some urgency it should be practised until the difficulties
arising out of towing a loaded dinghy have been identified and
overcome. With a rigid dinghy the problem is straightforward
because the boat's stability can be felt, nothing unexpected

happens as long as sudden movements and changes of trim are avoided, and the need to reduce speed is plainly apparent. The greatest difficulty in fact is likely to be that of manhandling the boat while out of the water. An inflatable on the other hand which is normally so stable and buoyant may behave with disconcerting abruptness in what seems to be an uncharacteristic manner. Because of its shape and low freeboard even a lightly loaded inflatable can swamp when under tow and fill almost instantaneously. In its normal state it derives its phenomenal stability from its rapid response to any movement of the water in which it floats, but when swamped it responds instead to the movement of the great weight of water which is surging around inside it, and if it is being towed in this condition it may despite its enormous buoyancy take a sudden dive, washing or spilling out its occupants and imposing an immense strain on the painter. The menace of this behaviour lies in its unexpectedness so the speed should be kept down to the level that you have found will not result in swamping in the prevailing conditions.

When lying alongside in a strong wind or tideway, and whenever heavy weights are being moved into or out of the dinghy regardless of conditions, she should be secured in position by means of the painter and not by the hands of occupants for two

A capsizing force: the dinghy should be secured by the painter and not by the hands

Always place stores securely on deck or cockpit before leaving the
dinghy—unlike this man

reasons. Hands that are busy hanging on are otherwise immobilized, and the painter attached to the stem is less likely to exert a
capsizing force or to pull her athwart wind or tide than are the
arms of people sitting in the boat.

A dinghy stowed on deck can contribute to seaworthiness by
adding useful shelter and secure handholds, or it can be a
dangerous obstruction. It must be strongly secured otherwise it
may not only be lost but knock someone overboard or injure him
and damage itself or the yacht. The gripes and lashings which
hold a rigid dinghy on to its chocks are liable to be stretched
by additional loads when used as handholds or by having gear
temporarily wedged under them, so they need to be of ample
strength and checked regularly for tautness when on passage. If
an inflatable is carried inflated on deck its lightness and elasticity
simplify its secure stowage, but it still offers considerable resistance to wind and water, and may in addition shrink through
cooling or leakage and so slacken its lashings.

5

MACHINERY

The function of an auxiliary engine is to provide an alternative source of power and to keep the batteries charged so that its own starting equipment and a potentially vast range of electrical devices can be used. Its most necessary attribute is reliability, without which efficiency, economy and all other mechanical virtues are wasted. For a given design and construction the reliability of an engine depends on the manner in which it is operated and looked after and the circumstances in which it has to work. Unfortunately the marine environment is so hostile to engines and electrical equipment that they deteriorate more from exposure to it than they do from the wear and tear of normal use. There is nothing remarkable about an engine being willing to start when it has been running every day for six months, but if it starts first time after being idle for six months it will cause admiring comment and very likely a revelation of the care with which it was prepared to withstand the ravages of its long inactivity.

The main difference between maintaining an engine and maintaining a sailing rig is that while you can judge the condition of every part of your rigging and sails by sight and touch, the moving and wearing parts of an engine are concealed and you can only infer their state indirectly from its performance, its noises, smokes, smells and other external manifestations which often appear only when trouble is well developed. But in the same way that the rig can be relieved of unfair wear and tear through considerate handling and adherence to well thought out routines, the health of an engine can be preserved by following all the recommendations of the manufacturer's handbook and by devising and sticking to routines for starting, stopping and short-term maintenance.

All types of internal combustion engines need air, fuel, lubricants and coolant, which have to be clean and of the correct grade. The operating handbook gives information about the intervals at which filters and oil should be changed and a brief daily inspection will either confirm that all is well or reveal the first signs of trouble. The level of fuel in the tank should decrease at a rate proportional to the amount of work done by the engine, so check it every day. A level lower than expected indicates either abnormal fuel consumption or a leak; if it is higher something—probably water—is getting into the tank. A leaking fuel system is potentially dangerous. If the fuel is petrol an undiscovered leak could result in an explosion and fire when the engine is next started. With diesel fuel a second fault or incident would be needed before this could occur but the second fault could be there already, or be on the point of developing. Unsuspected contamination of fuel by water can be almost as nasty because the water lies in the sump of the tank until a rough sea stirs it up or it rises above the level of the feed-pipe and the engine stops. Similarly check the oil level in crankcase and gearbox. As well as making sure there is enough, this allows you to check consumption and gives a warning of contamination by fuel or water if there is too much. Either way it gives you a chance to pinpoint the trouble and cure it before damage is done. If there is a heat exchanger, checking the coolant level can give valuable information about the development of leaks into or out of the system.

After checking the levels, the outside of the engine and all its pipelines should be examined for leaks of fluids and gases. These are immediately apparent on clean surfaces but may not be detected if everything is covered with a mixture of oil and dust, so keep the engine clean. At the same time a general condition check of obvious items like drive belts can be made depending on the individual engine.

The object of starting and stopping routines is like any other drill to ensure that a sequence of operations including certain necessary functional checks is followed in the right order and without omission regardless of who does it, so that the engine is started successfully, mishaps are avoided, and sometimes so that the stage is set for the next operation. These routines can only be worked out in relation to specific engines, and even to individual installations, so the examples which follow are for illustration only.

Typical starting routine

1 If petrol engine, check no naked lights near engine compartment
2 Turn on fuel (if petrol, check fuel is present at carburettor)
3 Turn on cooling water
4 Open exhaust seacock
5 Set engine controls to starting positions
6 Select neutral gear and release shaft brake
7 Energize starter
8 When engine starts, check:
   (a) Oil pressure rises
   (b) Warning lights are out
   (c) Ammeter shows charge
   (d) Water appears at outlet

Typical stopping routine

1 Set recommended engine speed
2 Select neutral gear (may be unnecessary if gearbox is mechanically operated)
3 If petrol, turn off fuel at tank
   If diesel, operate stop control
4 When engine stops switch off alternator (ignition if petrol)
5 Close appropriate seacocks
6 Apply shaft brake

Whenever work is being done on a petrol engine there is a possibility that fuel vapour may be released. As the smallest spark of flame is capable of igniting this, precautions have to be taken to ensure that depending on the nature of the work there is neither petrol vapour nor the chance of a spark present. To do this stop the engine by closing the valve at the tank while the engine is still running so that it empties the carburettor, then disconnect the battery and short out the magneto. You should also prohibit smoking and naked lights anywhere on board unless the boat is large and the engine compartment sufficiently isolated in which case it may suffice to restrict the prohibited area to the engine room.

If the defect is in the fuel system and it is necessary to run fuel through it in the course of rectification the electrical and ignition systems should on no account be re-connected until any spills have been dried up and the whole area including communicating bilges thoroughly ventilated.

Operating or testing electrical components should only be done in the absence of fuel. It is safe to short out the sparking plugs of a running engine, but dangerous to check the spark by turning the engine over with the plugs removed and earthed, and extremely dangerous to disconnect electrical leads from the engine without having first disconnected the battery.

These precautions should be embodied in a routine or drill which—like the starting and stopping routines—should be written down so that anyone can refer to it.

Diesel engines have the advantage of using a fuel that does not vaporize unless heated, and of being independent of damp-shy electrical ignition systems so their operation and maintenance is more straightforward. Vigilance to detect early signs of trouble and careful adherence to the manufacturer's recommendations are again the best guarantee of reliability.

It has to be remembered that power failure can occur through no fault of the engine itself. Starting batteries can run down or fail, gearboxes are subject to a variety of ills, propellers can be fouled or come loose on the shaft, so your reliance on power depends on the reliability of the whole system from the fuel filler deckplate to the exhaust skin-fitting, from the cooling water inlet to the split-pin in the propellor nut.

Attitude to repairs and to the range of spares and tools carried vary with the capability of the individual, the importance he attaches to having auxiliary power, and the extent to which he must rely on the yacht's own resources. A skipper contemplating a distant cruise off a thinly inhabited coast might count on finding less skilled help and fewer spare parts than if he were marina-hopping along the south coast of England, on the other hand he might find power failure so much less of a handicap that he could accept the risk of being unable to cure it. Whatever the circumstances there is little point in carrying spare parts and tools for jobs that are beyond the yacht's own skill and resources unless she is embarking on a cruise to an area in which skilled help is obtainable but the spares have to be specially ordered and imported.

Sea water and electricity form such a destructive combination that all marine electrical installations need careful planning and constant inspection if damage both to themselves and their surroundings are to be avoided. In electrical terms the whole of the exterior and much of the interior of a yacht is a *submarine* environment. As most electrical fittings are so constructed that when water has once got into them it tends to remain there they either need to be waterproofed which is in many cases impossible, or sited where water cannot reach them. Switches, light-sockets and all breakable connections are particularly vulnerable, moving parts and the tiny set-screws of terminals being the first components to succumb through seizure or disintegration. Static components can be protected in cooler climates by a liberal application of lanolin and it is sometimes possible to enclose a switch completely in a permanent waterproof cover that is flexible enough to allow operation through the cover itself. So called 'watertight' fittings are seldom more than weatherproof which means that they are suitable for exposed positions below decks such as the vicinity of hatches, but not on deck or in the cockpit unless given the protection of a locker or ventilator box.

Batteries need to be arranged to provide a reserve of power so that the engine can be started regardless of other demands on the system. The most versatile method is to duplicate the power supply so that either set can be brought into circuit for all purposes; alternatively one set can be used solely for starting and services that are used only while the engine is running, while the other is used for all other purposes.

PART II
HANDLING

6

HANDLING UNDER POWER

Note For the sake of clarity it is assumed throughout this chapter that the propeller is right-handed (ie when viewed from aft it rotates clockwise) and is located on the yacht's centreline forward of the rudder. When the principles discussed here have been understood there should be no difficulty in applying them to alternative installations.

When a boat is under power three factors combine to foster an impression that control is easier and more certain than when she is sailing:

1 Power is available either ahead or astern regardless of the direction of the vessel's head.
2 The amount of power can be adjusted at will simply by moving a lever.
3 Slipstream from the propeller passing over the rudder renders it effective even when the boat has no forward way.

This impression will be illusory unless two other factors, the effect of wind and the turning effects of the propeller, are taken into consideration. They need to be looked at separately.

The effect of wind
Try the following experiment: in sheltered water and moderate wind (force 4 is ideal), with sails stowed take all way off the boat without using power, leave the helm free and watch what happens. Unless she is of unusual design she will pivot round until the

wind is well abaft the beam, maybe even dead astern, gather way and then begin to luff. After this different types of boat behave in a variety of ways and you will have to see what yours does, allowing plenty of time for her to stabilize either on a steady heading or in a repeating cycle of movements. Repeat several times to check consistency of results.

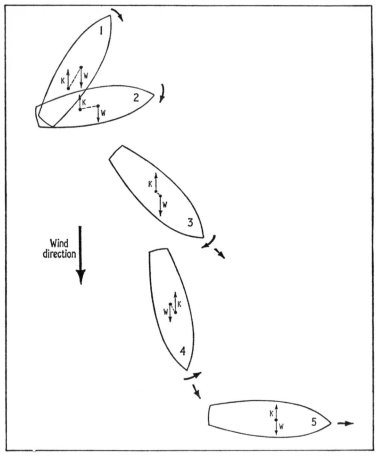

Drifting under bare poles: (1 and 2) stopped and turning. K is the keel force, W the wind force; (3) gathering way. Still turning as speed increases, K moves forward; (4) still accelerating but beginning to turn back into the wind because the W/K couple has reversed; (5) forereaching slowly on a steady heading when W and K coincide

When a sailing boat is completely stopped with no sail set the windage of the hull and rig is centred somewhat forward of amidships and well forward of the centre of resistance of her submerged parts; in consequence she turns downwind. This brings the resistances into line so that there is no longer any tendency to turn and she straightens up stern-to-wind. In this attitude water resistance is greatly reduced, wind resistance only slightly so, and she gathers way. Forward movement through the water causes the centre of water resistance to move forward and overtake the centre of wind resistance (which itself moves aft because the bows are now sheltered). This creates an unstable situation in which the smallest yaw is enough to initiate a turn back into wind. During the turn the bow becomes more and more exposed to the wind, moving the centre of wind pressure forward nearer to the centre of water pressure and so decreasing the turning moment. Once the boat has turned approximately through a right angle the wind is trying to drive her more sideways than forward and leeway develops. Leeway slows the boat down by increasing water resistance and at the same time causes the centre of water pressure to move still further forward, thus tending to maintain the turn into wind.

What happens after this depends on the individual boat. One may luff so much that she loses way altogether and then pays off stern-to-wind to begin the whole cycle all over again. Another may luff more and more slowly until she achieves a stable balance forereaching across the wind at a constant speed and angle. Others may achieve this state after a series of damping oscillations.

The initial yaw away from the wind when the boat is stopped is the most crucial of the effects of wind where handling under power is concerned, but observation of the entire pattern provides useful knowledge.

Effect of the propeller

The next experiment must be made in calm conditions so that the results are not confused by the effects of wind, preferably in slack water and certainly clear of eddy currents. With the boat

stopped line up a mark dead ahead and keeping the helm amidships open up to cruising power ahead. She will almost certainly
yaw off the mark and if uncorrected will continue the turn in the
same direction. Which way is she turning? Straighten up on a
mark, reduce power and with helm amidships once more engage
astern gear and increase power. Notice the yaw in the opposite
direction and as the boat gathers sternway try to control her
with rudder. How fast does she need to be moving before she will
answer? How does the thrust from the propeller when going astern
compare with that going ahead?

If your boat has a right-handed propeller, the yaw will have
been anticlockwise when going ahead (bow swings to port),
clockwise when going astern (stern swings to port). This is
because the thrust of the propeller is not straight ahead or astern
but obliquely across the boat's fore and aft axis. The simplest
explanation is that since the blades moving around the lower part
of their rotational path do so in denser water than those moving
in the opposite direction across the top, the torque reaction is
unbalanced and the propeller behaves like a paddle-wheel whose
lower blades are working in a denser medium (water) than the
upper ones which are in air. This is sometimes known as
'paddle-wheel effect'. The fact that the small propeller of a yacht's
auxiliary produces more paddle-wheel effect than would be expected can be explained by the rake of the shaft (usual in such
installations to improve propeller immersion) causing the down-
going blades to exert more thrust than the upgoing ones when
driving ahead and vice versa when going astern. The effect of this
is to reinforce the paddle-wheel effect.

One further effect from the propeller may be evident. We
noticed that although the engine seemed less powerful when going
astern the tendency to yaw was as great or even greater than when
going ahead. The loss of power is partly because more is dissipated
in the gearbox, but chiefly because the propeller which is designed
for thrusting ahead becomes extremely inefficient when its blade
sections are turned back to front and upside-down in going astern.
This decrease in thrust is not accompanied by a corresponding
increase in torque which is likely to be as high or even higher,

so that when going astern the yaw becomes more noticeable.

When these effects are understood and we are familiar with their manifestations in an individual boat they cease to be alarming and subversive; we can not only allow for them but make use of them as the next two experiments will demonstrate.

Turning short round

Aim: to turn the boat through 360° in the least possible space. Conditions: slack water; little or no wind.

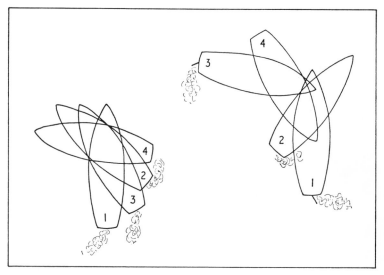

Turning in a confined space: propeller effect when going astern favours the turn to starboard

Preliminaries: find a quiet corner and if no convenient marker such as a vacant mooring exists, anchor a buoy to serve as a reference point. Steady the boat on a landmark and take all way off. Apply full starboard helm, engage forward gear, open up smoothly to cruising revolutions, then turn through 360° and steady on the original mark at the same time taking off the power. Estimate the diameter of the turning circle. Repeat the manoeuvre exactly, but this time turning to port. You now know in which direction the tightest turn can be made using rudder alone.

65

It is most likely to be the same as the direction in which the propeller caused yaw when going ahead in our earlier experiment, ie to port if the propeller is right-handed. Do not be dismayed if it is not because if the propeller effect is small in your boat it could be masked by other factors, and it does not invalidate the main part of the experiment, which follows.

Line the boat up on the original mark and stop her a few yards from the buoy. Turn her round to port using short bursts of power ahead and astern together with full helm. Use power liberally, but reduce and then reverse it as soon as the boat begins to gather way in either direction. Concentrate on turning the boat as nearly as possible on one spot and count the number of times you change from ahead to astern. Notice that going ahead, the combined influences of helm and propeller turn her very readily to port but that when going astern the rudder is powerless to counteract propeller effect which tends to straighten the boat up and may even start a turn to starboard.

When you have completed the turn straighten up on the original mark and repeat, this time turning to starboard. Notice that the boat continues to turn in the right direction both when going ahead and astern and that the manoeuvre is completed in less time and with fewer reversals of thrust.

Berthing alongside

Aim: to position the boat with way off in a chosen alongside berth, roughly parallel to it, without touching but close enough for a crew member to step ashore.

Conditions: slack water; wind not more than force 3; direction immaterial as long as it does not make the berth on lee shore. The berth you have chosen is approximately twice the overall length of your boat, and the berths ahead and astern are both occupied. The occupants may be imagined until you have gained confidence, but play fair or the experiment will be wasted. Think the procedure out from what you know already.

The occupied berths dictate an oblique approach, while the shortness of the berth demands that you straighten up and stop in one movement. There being no stream you can approach either way and clearly the best way is port side to, so rig fenders and lines and have a go. As everything is working for you, you can afford to come in at a good big angle, allowing ample clearance between the moored boat on the approach side and your stern which will swing towards her as you put the engine astern. Approach in neutral at the least speed that will give positive rudder control; use the helm to start turning as soon as you see that your stern will clear your neighbour and go astern firmly on the engine, decreasing power as headway is killed and returning to neutral when parallel to the dockside. If she starts to gather sternway before you are parallel a brief burst ahead against full helm will check it and straighten her up.

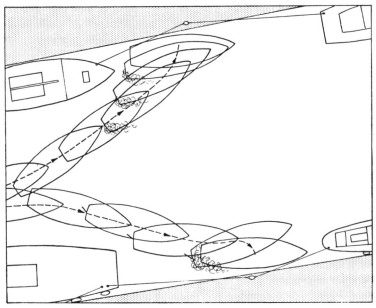

Berthing alongside: allowing for the swing caused by putting the engine astern

The trickiest part of this operation is likely to have been keeping your eye on the ball while manipulating the engine controls. It is of course essential to be able to do this without looking at them, but the siting of engine controls in a sailing cockpit is

67

governed by so many considerations unconnected with their actual use that it is often necessary to stoop at the very least in order to reach them and the helmsman may be unsighted for a few crucial seconds. Practice helps more than anything, but there may be scope for ingenuity, adaptation, the acquisition of new skills of knee or foot.

The next part of the exercise is to repeat the manoeuvre from the opposite direction so that you finish up lying starboard side to. In planning the manoeuvre you will have to allow for the yaw to starboard that will occur when you put the engine astern, so you must use the rudder to turn the boat in the berth until she is pointing somewhat outwards, taking care not to swing the stern against the dockside. Compared with the earlier manoeuvre this needs much more accurate judgement throughout and the feeling of control is less confident.

Control under power is very largely a matter of making use of the yawing effects of wind and propeller, using the one to help or oppose the other as appropriate. In a strong wind for instance it may be much easier to berth alongside or bring up to a buoy heading downwind because when stopped the boat will not have the tendency to turn round which can demand such a tricky balancing act when head-to-wind. One of the easiest ways of maintaining a stopped position in a fresh breeze is to go astern with just enough power to prevent the boat being blown ahead by the wind.

The effect of tide

Although a boat is affected by tide in the same way whether she is sailing or under power more people appear to experience difficulty from this source when motoring than they do when sailing. Perhaps we take more careful note of what the tide is doing when under sail.

A tidal stream is almost always helpful when manoeuvring as long as we can head into it, unhelpful when we get athwart it or bring it astern. When stemming a stream it is possible to maintain steerage way and full control down to zero speed over the ground, and even while dropping astern if the stream is strong

Vertue XXXV, one of the best known of her famous class, originally designed by Laurent Giles and Partners in the 1930s. This seaworthy 25-footer has accomplished numerous ocean voyages and given much pleasure to many 'ordinary families' (*Eric C. Hiscock*)

Another highly successful design by Laurent Giles, the Westerly Centaur carries a much lighter rig than the Vertue reflecting the difference in displacement, but her shallower hull has required a high cabin-top for the sake of full headroom (*Gilbert le Cossec, Revue Bateaux*)

enough. The only problem likely to be met is that of swirls and eddies but even so control is easiest and manoeuvrability greatest when stemming the stream. This is simply demonstrated by comparing the ease with which an obstruction can be avoided when stemming a foul tide to the hair-raising business of dodging one when the tide is under you. This leads to one of the few general rules that can be applied in boat handling. Always bring up to a fixed object bows on to the stream. This often involves turning round from an initially downstream approach which can create unwelcome drama unless it is properly thought out, as the following example shows. As shown on p 73, your boat is approaching her mooring on a strong flood stream. The mooring is in mid-channel where the stream is strongest and near the upstream end of an area which is fairly congested with moored yachts. Twenty yards further upstream is a clear space and thirty yards beyond that the whole river is obstructed by a solid mass of small boat moorings. The swift stream in the centre of the channel is bordered on both sides by areas of almost slack water extending some ten to fifteen yards within the navigable limits, which are two and a half times the diameter of your turning circle apart. How are you going to get onto your mooring?

You rightly decide that you must turn round and approach it from down-tide. There is a space just big enough to turn in without risk of being set athwart any moorings while you do it, but you will have to turn very smartly to avoid being carried up amongst the small boats. The most direct route is to approach up the edge of the channel, outside all the moorings and round up in a tight turn onto your own buoy. Alternatively you could come up in mid-channel through the moored boats, turn towards the bank as soon as you are clear, and then work back across the tide to mid-stream and back to the mooring. Since you can choose to turn port or starboard on either plan this gives you four choices. Think it over.

Picking up man overboard
This manoeuvre needs to be tested, adapted and thoroughly rehearsed. If you are motoring in a calm the quickest way back

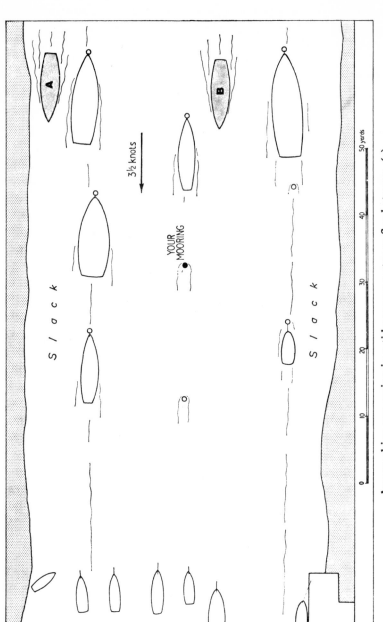

Approaching a mooring in a tideway on a strong flood stream, (1)

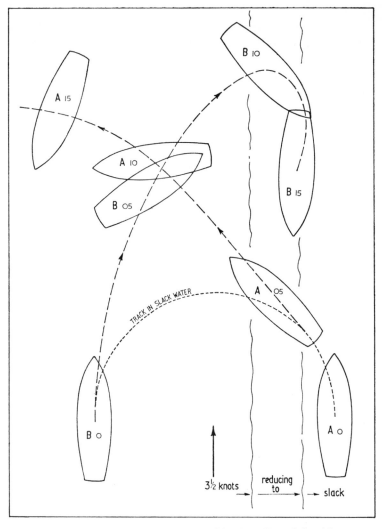

Approaching a mooring in a tideway, (2); the effect of the tide on a
turn that would take A or B round a semi-circle in slack water in
fifteen seconds. Positions are plotted at five-second intervals from
the two starting points A and B. The effect of changing power may
be imagined in these two cases and their mirror images

to the man in the water is to put on full helm to starboard and go astern on the engine until he is straight ahead of you. Approach near enough to bring the man within reach and abeam, slow down and *stop the engine*. Not only will there be ropes in the water but a rotating propeller is an appalling menace to anyone alongside, and the inevitable scrambling about raises the risk of the controls being accidentally moved if the gear is merely put into neutral. The only way to be sure that the propeller cannot rotate is to shut down the engine completely.

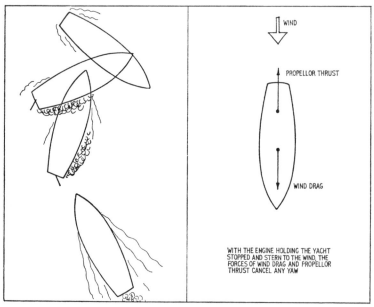

WIND

PROPELLOR THRUST

WIND DRAG

WITH THE ENGINE HOLDING THE YACHT STOPPED AND STERN TO THE WIND, THE FORCES OF WIND DRAG AND PROPELLOR THRUST CANCEL ANY YAW

An emergency about-turn and lying stopped under power

If there is a wind try circling upwind and approaching with the wind aft, going astern on the engine to bring the boat to a stop. The boat will lie more steadily stern on to wind and sea and the final approach with engine going astern is safer because the propeller wash is pushing the man away instead of sucking him in as it does when going ahead. Remember to stop the engine as soon as possible, and if you find this manoeuvre does not work well with your boat experiment until you find one which does.

Leaving an alongside mooring

In the absence of tidal stream or onshore wind, getting away from a berth alongside is simply a matter of applying what we have already discovered, but plan each step first and have ready everything that will be needed. Circumstance will usually indicate whether it is better to leave bow or stern first and which mooring lines can be unrigged in the process of singling up. If the wind cannot be used to slant the bow out from the dockside you can go gently astern or ahead against a spring to swing the bow or stern out, but be ready with a fender as the opposite end swings in.

If there is an onshore wind pressing the boat against the dockside the task becomes more difficult. With a wind at an oblique angle it may be possible to swing bow or stern through it or at least into it, otherwise the most hopeful method is to get the bow turned well out and lose no time in gaining full steerage way. The worst situation is to have to leave stern foremost when lying starboard side to, and it may be necessary to warp her clear or haul off to an anchor.

A stream from ahead is as usual an advantage as the boat can be underway and fully under control before the last of the mooring lines are slipped. If on the other hand you are lying stern on to a stream you need to be perfectly confident of your ability to control the yacht when making sternway. If there is any doubt it is better to time your departure for slack water or turn the boat round in her berth at the previous slack so that she is facing into the stream that will be running when you leave.

Power failure

There are so many reasons, not all of them relating to the engine, why a yacht should suddenly find herself deprived of power that the possibility has to be allowed for whenever she is motoring. Only in exceptional circumstances is power failure itself an emergency, but an emergency may well arise out of the crew's inability to foresee and cope with the consequences. Power failure in the open sea and clear of traffic is unlikely to require rapid decisions or urgent action: the yacht might drift safely for hours or even days while making repairs or waiting for wind. In the outer part of a harbour she might have ample time to make sail if there is wind or to bring her dinghy into service as a tug if it is calm.

When the yacht loses her propulsion in a confined space your speed of reaction will be a lot quicker if you have sized up the situation beforehand and anticipated what you need to do. The first priority is to avoid hitting anything; the second is to use the boat's momentum to gain a position of maximum advantage while she still has steerage way; the third is to prevent her from drifting into danger. In some situations all three aims can be achieved by a single action, but the only way to give yourself a reasonable chance of a successful outcome without hair-raising incidents is to include the idea of an escape route in your moment-by-moment planning and have all the necessary gear ready for immediate use.

7

HANDLING UNDER SAIL

When a yacht is on passage in the open sea the aim in handling her is usually to make progress towards an objective. This is achieved by striking a balance between speed, reasonable living and working conditions for the crew, steadiness and balance on the helm, and moderation of stress on hull and rig. Though events and circumstances may alter the relative priorites of these factors and introduce new ones, the basic concern is to maintain speed and direction.

In restricted waters the principal aim of handling is to manoeuvre, to be able to change speed and direction. Speed becomes important more for its effect on the yacht's ability to manoeuvre than for the distance she can cover in a given time; the crew's endurance becomes less critical than its muscle power; and sails are likely to be chosen more with an eye to what the crew can handle smartly than to what the yacht can comfortably carry.

Since the considerations involved in manoeuvring are the more basic and since you can hardly get to sea without having first been in harbour we shall begin by investigating manoeuvre, the control of speed and direction.

Manoeuvring under sail
There are two entirely distinct aspects of the technique of manoeuvring depending on whether the boat has steerage way or not. As long as she has steerage way a boat can be controlled by movement of her rudder and adjustment to the trim of her sails, and the higher her speed the greater the effect of a given rudder deflection. In the absence of steerage way the rudder is ineffective

77

so the sails alone must be used to control direction. (The use of oars, lines, quants and so on has been left out of this discussion in order to concentrate more precisely on the problems of handling under sail.) The directional control of a boat is easier, more straightforward and less liable to be upset by fluctuations of wind direction or strength if her pace is brisk rather than slow, but since many manoeuvres begin or end with the boat stopped we must have control over the whole range of speed, and also have to retain control of direction in the absence of steerage way.

The first requirement for successful manoeuvring is to have the right amount of sail. Too little sail results in inadequate speed for positive control, uncertainty in stays, lack of momentum to carry way through lulls or to luff past obstructions. Too much makes heavier work of steering and sail handling, increases heel angle and requires more space for losing way. The ideal sail plan for manoeuvre is that which has enough total area to give a lively response on all points of sailing, and is made up of sails that can be easily and smartly handled. It is easier to reduce speed by sailing inefficiently than it is to compensate for inadequate power.

Yachts vary so much and are subject to so many changing influences that it is impossible to have stereotyped sets of instructions for carrying out different manoeuvres. You cannot even say for instance that hardening in the mainsheet always causes a boat to luff; it may be true for this one; that one may luff if she is moving but bear away if she is stopped; another may luff at first but cease to do so if the sail is flattened beyond a certain point. The only way to find out is by experiment with the individual boat. Once the general handling characteristics of a boat are familiar all kinds of evolutions can be attempted and perfected by practice, but the unthinking application of rule of thumb often leads to the situation in which men appear to be struggling with an unhandy recalcitrant boat. The aim of the following experiments is to discover her natural tendencies so that you can get her to work for you.

1 *Stopping* With the wind force 3–4, and working sails, approach a reference marker (lay your own if necessary) and when close to

it luff head to wind. Let fly all sheets and use rudder to keep her in the eye of the wind as long as you can, but let go the helm when it is no longer effective. Notice:

(a) What helm movements are needed to keep straight.
(b) How far she shoots before losing way.
(c) The subsequent behaviour of the boat.

The answer to (a) may be that it is enough to hold the helm amidships or it may be that you need to juggle, making increasingly large corrections as the speed falls off. A long thin heavy boat is likely to shoot further than a short fat light one, and you might find that she lies head-to-wind more steadily and even makes a sternboard before paying off. Most boats will eventually lie more or less stopped athwart the wind and drifting: their movements in reaching this attitude are worth noting and so is the direction and rate of drift which can be judged by eye from your reference marker.

2 *Effect of sail trim* Now, without touching the helm haul in the mainsheet until the sail is just full, and while she gathers way continue to adjust the sheet so as to keep the sail correctly trimmed. If she luffs head-to-wind keep the main pinned in long enough for you to observe her behaviour before letting it fly and returning to the original attitude. If the yacht does not come head-to-wind but stabilizes on a steady heading try the effect of altering the trim of the mainsail. Repeat for each individual sail in turn and then for all together, using helm if necessary to return to the stopped position which is the starting point for each part of the exercise.

3 *Maximum turn with minimum way* The aim of this experiment is to turn right round in the smallest possible space. Stop the boat head-to-wind, use every possible sail and helm adjustment, and making a sternboard if necessary, pay off and keep turning. If she will come right up into the wind it ought to be possible to keep the turn going indefinitely, but if she sticks before completing the first 360° get her turning in the opposite direction and alter your tactics to see if you can effect any improvement.

4 *Sailing slowly* Reduce speed by incorrectly trimming the sails, easing sheets to spill wind when close-hauled or close-reaching, pinning them in when broad-reaching and running. See how slowly you can sail without losing positive control. One of the most essential bits of knowledge for close quarters manoeuvring is the boat's critical speed for tacking. This is the lowest speed at which she is capable of going about with certainty, but remember that the result will have to be adjusted for different conditions because a stronger wind or bigger sea will slow the boat more in stays and so raise the critical speed.

5 *Manoeuvring under a single sail* The ability to handle under a single sail when the wind is strong enough to make its area adequate is a great advantage, but as there may be unforeseen effects to cope with, it should first be practised where there is plenty of room, and remember that most difficulties that arise when manoeuvring under sail do so because the speed is allowed to get too low and that these difficulties are usually harder to get out of if you have only one sail set. If the boat seems unresponsive under main only it may help if she is sailed fuller with a freer sheet.

Many modern boats sail better under headsail alone provided it can be tacked without risk of a snarl-up and sheeted home without delay. The advantage compared with the mainsail is in the ease with which it can be set or lowered on any point of sailing, the disadvantage is that you lose the clear foredeck and there may be a few moments while gathering way when she pays off uncontrollably.

Once a yacht's behaviour and capability under sail has been properly understood and experience has sharpened judgement, great precision is possible, and the only serious problem regularly encountered is the effect of fluke winds. Getting a strong puff broad on the quarter just when you have luffed to take a mooring can demand not only an urgent signal to the foredeck to abandon the evolution but an instant decision on where to go. There must never be nowhere for you to go on these occasions, and planning the escape route should be part and parcel of your overall plan just as it was when handling under power.

Having mastered the handling of an individual yacht under sail you can tackle any specific evolution according to what you have discovered about her responses and the prevailing conditions. It would be quite wrong to lay down programmes for the various evolutions and then try to force the boat into this set pattern. However, there are certain points to be borne in mind.

Effect of streams

The effect of strong streams on the apparent wind has to be allowed for. A typical example is that of a boat about to get away from a mooring at which a strong stream and a light wind are

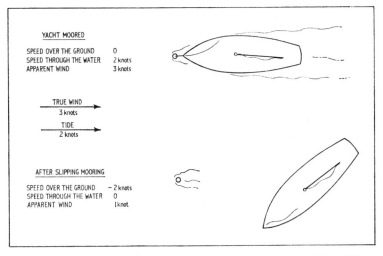

YACHT MOORED

SPEED OVER THE GROUND	0
SPEED THROUGH THE WATER	2 knots
APPARENT WIND	3 knots

TRUE WIND
3 knots

TIDE
2 knots

AFTER SLIPPING MOORING

SPEED OVER THE GROUND	– 2 knots
SPEED THROUGH THE WATER	0
APPARENT WIND	1 knot

The effect of strong streams on the apparent wind has to be allowed for

both in the same direction. She sets her sails, finds that there is enough wind to fill them, slips the buoy and behold! the wind miraculously dies away to nothing and she is swept out of control on the tide. In fact the true wind has remained constant but the tide carrying the yacht to leeward has made her apparent wind equal to the true wind minus the speed of the stream.

When beating with the tide up a channel look out for slacker streams or even counter-currents at the sides of the channel and go about before crossing into them, otherwise you may find your bow held in slack water while your stern is still being carried upstream.

Short tacking

When beating in a really narrow channel, momentum is your biggest asset so concentrate on keeping up the speed rather than on sailing close to the wind.

As you will be gaining ground to windward anyway while in stays you can afford to sail free and fast for the sake of better control and a reserve of speed to take care of heading puffs. Beware particularly of losing speed through pinching toward the end of tacks.

Coming to a buoy

Look at similar boats on adjacent moorings for indications of strength and direction of stream and make the final approach against it under appropriate rig. If there is no tide approach head-to-wind. Either way plan what to do if you miss. If the yacht still

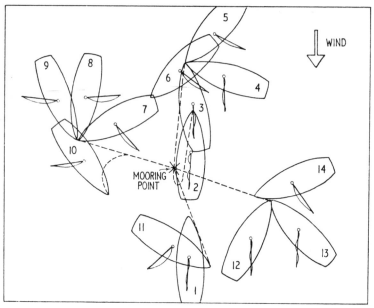

The effect of a slack mainsheet on a clumsy moor—the cause of many unseemly dramas

has way on after the mooring has been secured she may be snubbed round stern-to-wind, so either get the mainsail down smartly or pin it in tight amidships to kill its drive. A slack mainsheet in this situation has been the cause of many unseemly dramas and much slapping of spectators' thighs. When the wind is so strong against the tide that even bare poles give you too much speed you can slow down by making 'S' turns.

Berthing alongside

If the berth you intend to lie in lacks an escape route or is awkward to approach, choose a more convenient one in which to secure initially and warp into your final one afterwards. If you cannot approach head-to-wind or nearly so you will need to stow the mainsail and come in under headsail, dowsing it when you can carry your way into the berth.

The hot seat

Connected with the subject of manoeuvring in confined spaces and the need to base quick decision on accurate judgement are two schools of thought artificially opposed because both are perfectly right up to the point where their protagonists deny the validity of the alternative. On the one hand it is said that the skipper should be at the helm whenever the yacht is at close quarters so that he can detect the response and translate his own intentions directly into action without the need to communicate with a helmsman, and on the other that he should not be on the helm because the exercise of his command is hampered by his being tied to one spot and absorbed in one task. The existence of these two points of view is to be expected because to some people the helm is not only the mechanism that moves the rudder but an instrument through which they sense the movements and responses of the boat. To them 'handling' means using the sense of touch to feel and move something: not to have the boat under their own hand is to be deprived of a major means of perception. Others, to whom a tiller is no more than a lever, might just as well get someone else to work it provided he can be relied on to do as he is told, but they need to make compensatory use of their eyes and their intelligences and to make sure that their communications are loud and clear and absolutely unambiguous.

To appreciate the problem, imagine that you are in a ketch beating up an estuary, and having just gone about at the edge of the channel need to bear away to pass astern of a yacht on the starboard tack which is coming up fast on your lee bow. The helm is put over but nothing happens. If you are the helmsman how quickly do you know whether the steering gear has broken, the mizzen is sheeted a-weather, or the keel is ploughing a furrow in the mud? How quickly can you do anything about it? If someone else is steering what must you do to sort out the situation if (a) he says 'she won't answer', (b) he says nothing but with clenched jaw and reddening neck tries to force the helm past the limit?

Of course an enormous amount depends on the calibre of the helmsmen in your crew but your very first exercise of command is to allow no-one to dictate to you in this matter but do whatever suits your own nature best, and develop to your utmost ability the skills appropriate to your method.

Handling on passage

When a yacht is in open water and clear of dense traffic the need for manoeuvrability is only of prime importance in bad visibility and in unusual circumstances such as threatened collision, man overboard or involvement in another vessel's emergency. Naturally the aim will be to reach a destination in good time without subjecting crew or boat to strains beyond their capacity to sustain, and in these circumstances crew and boat give all the indications needed as to how she should be sailed. The right amount of sail is that which gives good progress with easy steering and motion, the boat feels happy and her crew both on watch and off sense this and are relaxed. Too little sail results in loss of swing and stride, a flawed metre in the poetry of motion, and a pervading sense of unease that becomes most pronounced in a flat calm. If overcanvassed the boat is usually first to complain when on the wind, the crew when running. Provided that the gear is strong enough an overpressed boat on the wind behaves in the way the old sailormen described with such precision, she labours: her dance resembles that of a man carrying a sack of coal, and the shocks of her burdened gait bring tension to her people's muscles and anxiety to the edges of their minds. Carrying too much sail when running demands acute concentration and sometimes physical exertion from helmsmen, causing them to tire quickly and steer inaccurate courses; and it may require an alteration of heading to one that can be held without risk of an accidental gybe. The skipper may fail to detect the signs unless he watches for them or reminds the helmsman to speak up if things become difficult. If he suspects but is not sure that a sail reduction or change of heading is needed he should take the helm himself for a short spell.

The bearing of circumstance on the question of what sail to set can be illustrated by comparing two boats, neither of which is racing, each carrying all she can stand in the same strong breeze. The first, her crew fresh after an easy passage, driving towards the lee of the land with a sheltered haven only hours away is giving her people the sail of their lives and they are revelling in it. The second, setting out with a two hundred mile passage ahead of her is giving hers a rough ride, the exhilaration they felt at the outset soon to be eroded by strain and fatigue, her skipper on a razor's edge expecting always the increase in wind or sea that will be the signal for shortening sail.

The ability to sail slowly or stop is just as useful on passage as it is in harbour. It may be prudent when approaching certain coasts to delay making a landfall until visibility improves; you may want to have an hour or so's respite from an uncomfortable thresh in order to prepare and eat a meal in peace or tackle a repair; a head sea may be giving you such a hammering that you have to stop and wait for wind and sea to moderate, or you may just want to stop for a chat. Whatever the reason the essential features of heaving to are that the yacht's forward way should be extremely slow and that she should lie on a steady heading with the helm unattended. The traditional method of backing a headsail works admirably in boats of heavy displacement with deep forefoot and long keel, but is seldom satisfactory in modern yachts except in light winds; in strong winds they tend to go too fast or to yaw wildly. Experiment is needed to find out what is best for a given yacht in different conditions and it must be remembered that what works in force 3 will probably not have the same effect in a gale. It may be best to begin strong wind experiments by sailing close-hauled under a single sail, either close-reefed mainsail, trysail, or a small headsail. When going to windward sail set aft of the mast produces less leeway and is more likely to keep the boat on a steady heading relative to the wind than one set forward of it, but in the case of a cutter the staysail might give the best results. It is not necessary to wait until it blows force 8 before making this experiment, valuable experience will be gained if the wind is strong enough to reduce you to close-reefed mainsail.

The trysail is usually thought of as a storm sail and consequently is stuffed away out of sight and is rarely if ever set. This is waste of a good sail because a trysail, being loosefooted, is extremely useful when off the wind in a rough sea even when the wind is no more than fresh, taking the sting out of accidental gybes, and allowing headsails to fill on a dead run when a mainsail would blanket them, yet supplying the steadying effect of a mainsail when headsails alone would cause unpleasant rolling. In some yachts it is not possible to arrange a satisfactory lead for the trysail sheet so its close-hauled performance may be poor. A trysail cannot be considered to be a storm sail unless it can be bent on and set in a gale. If this operation entails feeding the luff slides into the main track at arms length above the stowed mainsail the odds are it will seldom be attempted, and it would be better to have a really deep reef in the mainsail instead.

With modern rigs of high aspect ratio and very small mainsails the trysail would seem to have little function other than to act as a spare mainsail, so the cost and stowage space might be more usefully devoted to a second mainsail, and a small headsail set close to the mast as the storm sail. Large mainsails and long booms on the other hand make a trysail well worthwhile especially if it is of ample size and provided with a reef. Ideally it should have its own mast-track or at least a separate section, low enough for a sitting man to feed in the luff slides, and provided with a switch to connect it with the mainsail track.

The cockpit of this Westerly Conway affords good protection and an excellent all-round view. Her admirably clear decks are provided with 6 correctly placed mooring cleats (*J. A. Hewes*)

Securing the coil of a halyard to its cleat after it has been made fast (*New Glénans Sailing Manual, Editions du Seuil and David & Charles*)

PART III
PASSAGE MAKING

8

WATCHKEEPING

The purpose of watchkeeping is to ensure that the crew is fit to keep an alert look-out and work the ship efficiently for as long as she remains at sea. This is achieved by ensuring that the daily routine allows everyone enough time for sleeping, eating and recreation, so that efficiency is not reduced by fatigue or exposure. Every yacht that goes to sea ought to have a watchkeeping scheme ready and bring it into effect as soon as it is apparent that it will become necessary. The projected passage may be expected to last only eight or nine hours, but a necessary diversion or unexpected development could result in the yacht remaining at sea for many hours longer.

Working craft and racing yachts are usually manned in such a way that half the crew can work the ship while the other half is off-duty. In these circumstances the traditional system of two watches, taking turn and turn about every four hours, answers tolerably well although landsmen may take a few days to get used to this patchwork routine. Except in quiet weather the motion aboard a small yacht so hampers even simple actions that by the time a man has got out of his wet clothes, organized his bunk and visited the heads, he may barely have three hours of his watch below in his bunk before it is time for him to start getting dressed for the deck again.

Cruising yachts, being under less pressure to turn human effort into distance made good, can afford to take their deckwork more slowly, can anticipate the need to reduce sail, postpone action to increase it, and so operate with fewer people in a watch. Few need more than two men on watch, many manage successfully with only one. The ability to operate with smaller watches makes the three-watch system, in which watchkeepers have two spells off for every one on, attractive and possible. Three hours is a good duration for the watch in this system because it is not arduous even in cold weather or if a man is alone, and it gives six hours off which is ample without becoming tediously long. Four hours can be a long time for a man to be alone on watch and eight hours off is too much for all but the very young and the most ardent exponents of Egyptian PT.

The number and duration of watches and the number of hands in each depends primarily on how many watchkeepers are available for duty and how many are needed on deck at one time. Other factors which have to be taken into account are:

Crew   The experience, capability and fitness of each watch-keeper.

Ship   The ease with which the vessel can be worked.
        The degree of shelter afforded to the working watch.
        The number of berths which can be used at sea.

Circumstances   Climate and weather.
        Density of traffic.
        Pressure of navigational activity.

In considering how many people will be available, thought has to be given to the positions of the cook and the skipper. Though many people enjoy cooking now and then (or are at least prepared to put up with it), most detest doing it all the time—especially at sea—so it seems reasonable that the task should be undertaken in rotation by each member of the crew, and this can be incorporated in the watchkeeping routine. Even if one person is willing to do all the cooking he or she will want some fresh air and a chance to sail the boat occasionally, so the cook might take a couple of watches during the day but be excused the middle night watches if the strength of the crew allows.

Since the skipper needs to be able to come and go as events require, he really ought to be independent of the watchkeeping system; he can then act as permanent standby and lend support to a watch that is weak or hardpressed. There is, however, a

strong case for including the skipper in the watchkeeping roster
if it makes a three-watch system possible.

There is no law that says watches must be of any given duration
or even that all watches through the twenty-four hours should be
of equal length. They can and ought to be adjusted to suit conditions and the needs of individual crews, bearing in mind always the
purpose which the system serves. Thus one family crew devised
a system that gave each member a watch of different length. Ten-
year-old took a short spell after supper while Mother put six-
year-old into his bunk, then, relieved by Mother who was gasping
for some fresh air and peace and quiet, ten-year-old turned in.
Father—a partly converted single-hander—woke up to take the
midnight forecast and then took over for $5\frac{1}{2}$ hours while his wife
and children slept. At 0600 Mother roused ten-year-old, armed
him with a sandwich and sent him out to relieve Father while she
got breakfast.

Mother and children shared the watchkeeping during the
forenoon, Father and children the afternoon. Because ten-year-
old was capable of taking the helm for an hour or so without losing
interest and concentration, and because Mother was able to get
most of her sleep in the same time as the children, it worked well
and enabled that family to remain at sea for many days at a stretch
without fatigue or boredom.

Whatever system of watchkeeping is adopted punctilious time-
keeping is essential, and it ought to be a point of honour for everyone to take over on time. It is particularly important to resist the
temptation to postpone calling the relief watch. It may be a quiet
night and the watch on deck in no hurry to come below, or it may
be the others had a rough time on their previous watch—or were
late off because a sail change was made at the change-over. Whatever the reason, if the relief is called late they will in their turn
feel obliged to give their relief an extra five or ten minutes and the
whole system is then in danger of breaking up. There may be
occasions when a watch ought to be given a chance to catch up on
sleep, but this breaking of the routine should be done only on the
skipper's instructions and must not be passed on to succeeding
watches.

The mates of watches or watch leaders should have their duties clearly defined and be given specific instructions as to what tasks they are to undertake and the circumstances in which the skipper expects to be called. In all probability the skipper will have to issue separate orders to each individual to take account of variations in competence, aiming always to give as much scope and responsibility to each as his experience and ability justifies. The simplest method is to have standing orders to watch leaders permanently stuck inside the cover of the deck log book where all may refer to them and to supplement these with notes to individuals in the Remarks column.

Typical orders would define the watch leader's responsibility under the following headings:

1   *Lookout*: for other ships, obstructions, navigational marks, weather.
2   *Compliance with* IRPCS.
3   *Navigation*: maintaining course ordered; routine recording (at stated intervals) of log reading, course *steered* since last entry; incidental recording of time, log reading and details of any change of heading, marks sighted, etc.
4   *Seamanship*: security of gear; avoidance of chafe and damage; correct trim of sails; pumping of bilges at stated intervals and recording of number of strokes; avoid disturbing watch below with unnecessary noise.
5   *Occasions on which skipper is to be called*: accident to crew or damage to gear; ship on constant bearing within specified range; deterioration of weather especially visibility; anything which watch leader is unable to resolve or which worries him.

This last order should leave watch leaders in no doubt that the skipper would rather be called out for insufficient reason than be left until an emergency is well developed. It is a dreadful thing to stumble half awake into the cockpit while a ship rushes past only yards away because the watch were unsure of the danger but reluctant to disturb you; and it is essential that having made this point clear you never rebuke a man for rousing you unnecessarily.

Examples of specific instructions to individuals are that an inexperienced hand might be told to call the skipper if a wind-shift results in the yacht being headed more than twenty degrees, if another vessel approaches so closely that her sidelights become visible, and on sighting a navigational mark. A fully competent mate, on the other hand, might simply be left a note stating the critical angle for the current tack, and the intention to pass five miles off a certain headland.

9

NAVIGATING

There are no mysteries in navigation, no secrets revealed only to initiates. The simple theory and straightforward technique are open to anyone who has basic geography, elementary arithmetic and is prepared to study with a modicum of attention. Laying off a course, working up an estimated position or plotting a fix are in themselves no more difficult than any other task that has to be done while cruising, but just as cooking breakfast or adjusting the tension of a drive belt can, in a rough sea, demand all of a man's determination, concentration, resourcefulness and even physical strength, so can the navigator's task become one of extreme difficulty at just those times when speed and accuracy are vital.

The difference is that as long as a yacht is within about a day's sail of the land, navigating her is a continuous process requiring someone's constant attention and frequent activity.

Under good conditions a navigator can achieve encouragingly accurate results with just a little practice, but as soon as the sea begins to make itself felt, compass bearings can only be made approximately. Even the yacht's heading becomes a matter of estimation, and accuracy comes to mean how nearly you can assess the inaccuracies that exist and are unavoidable—the precision with which you can delineate your area of uncertainty. Hence the many tales about wise old navigators who put broad thumbs on the chart saying, 'We're about here' when the new boy has indicated the position with a point of the dividers.

As the person responsible for the efficient navigation of his ship the skipper will be at pains to reduce all sources of inaccuracy and to quantify what remains; but when he has swung the compass and calibrated the log and the DF, he has yet to tackle the sources of the most serious errors, himself and his crew.

Taking the navigator first. Mistakes arise most commonly in calculation and in plotting. He is most likely to make them, and most unlikely to spot them when he is tired, seasick, or when his concentration is broken. The obvious remedy is to guard against overwork, ensure that he gets proper food and rest, and has good working conditions.

The remainder of the crew are most likely to make mistakes in steering (or assessing the mean course they have been steering), and in recording information either by writing down wrong figures or failing to record all relevant facts such as the log reading at the time an alteration of course was made. Assuming that the watchkeeping and domestic arrangements are good enough to maintain the crew's fitness, a want of skill in steering can only be rectified by practice and its effects compensated for by supervision. Inadequately or wrongly recorded information is the bugbear of navigators and may be the result of slackness, lack of will, or failure to grasp the importance of the information.

All these sources of inaccuracy can be reduced at a stroke by involving more people in the job of navigating. If the skipper does all the navigating himself, he is not only overworked but exposed to the kind of conflict of priorities that can cause a serious error of judgement in an emergency. Ideally there ought to be in each watch a navigator capable of at least taking and plotting bearings and of working up the EP, and all watchkeepers should as a matter of course perform tasks like checking transits, taking compass bearings, etc. When the watchkeepers have a direct interest they are more likely to be diligent in the discharge of their navigational duties. Moreover, it is a great advantage in wet weather if a suitably clad man can take bearings in the cockpit for a dry navigator to plot rather than having a sodden navigator go below to drip all over the chart while his glasses mist up and he struggles to command obedience from cold and waterlogged fingers.

Naturally, the skipper must satisfy himself that the job is properly done, that standardized working methods provide a safeguard against confusion between individuals, and he must take the strategic decisions; but a part of his responsibility to his crew is to conserve his own fitness as well as theirs and another is ensure their ability to carry on if he gets put out of action. Neither is properly performed if he carries the whole navigational burden himself.

Turning to material considerations, a navigator needs equipment that will work for him and that he does not have to fight. His chart table may be a full-sized navigating desk or it may be only a piece of ply with elastic bands, but he must be able to adopt a comfortable working position, see what he is doing, and put down his tools without their scampering instantly out of sight like mice. The smaller the boat the more thought and ingenuity is needed to achieve good working conditions, and the greater the advantage of preliminary work both in the organizing of reference material and in actual plotting. Anything that can be done comfortably and at leisure in harbour has a better chance of being accurate and also relieves the work load under the more difficult conditions at sea.

Those who are mathematically inclined, or who enjoy playing with electronic calculators, may prefer to navigate by calculation rather than by plotting. The attractions are greater accuracy combined with minimal demands on space and equipment, but the advantages of plotting are that its graphic form makes immediate sense to anyone who looks at it and mistakes are revealed in true proportion. An error of calculation may pass unnoticed regardless of size unless deliberately sought out. A serious mistake in plotting will usually be glaringly obvious, one that is difficult to detect will be likely to be of small consequence, so even if calculation is used a plot should always be kept. All data should, in any event, be recorded in a separate notebook so that the working can be checked and a post-passage analysis made in pursuit of evidence with which to improve future accuracy.

Working through the navigation of a passage in advance is an extremely useful exercise for clarifying the navigator's aims, so that he knows for instance the stages when he needs fixes and where he ought to be working on limiting lines: it provides an invaluable guide to his briefing of watchkeepers and by habituating him to thinking ahead it helps the inexperienced to cross the gulf that separates classroom navigation from the real thing.

Just as the planning of a passage may show that the best route to your destination is not necessarily the most direct one, that the longer way round an intervening danger may be easier to follow, or that a landfall made some distance along the coast can make position fixing more certain, so the events of the passage can introduce the need to revise strategy as you go along.

This is particularly true of meteorological developments that affect visibility and wind. Even a very small weather system like a shower is so large and so fast-moving compared with a yacht that it is usually impossible to avoid altogether, but we can to some extent control the timing of the encounter and choose the ground on which it takes place.

Quiet anticyclonic conditions produce the sort of settled spell that tempts the smallest yachts to make a passage despite light winds and also favour the formation of radiation fog over the land at night. This fog may persist over estuaries and the coast during the early morning and even drift a little way out to sea, so if there are light winds and clear skies at night over your objective it is wise to time your landfall for the afternoon. Sea fog can occur with quite strong winds and persist for days until dispersed by the arrival of a drier or colder air mass, on some coasts there will be no alternative but to stand out to sea avoiding concentrations of traffic and wait for an improvement. In many places, however, it may be possible to approach the coast closely enough on a combination of soundings and radio bearings to find a safe anchorage. A close study of both chart and *Pilot* may reveal a better place for this than the landfall originally intended.

The low cloud and rain associated with troughs and the warm sector of a depression can make the approach to a coast that is fronted by off-lying dangers a nerve-wracking exercise. With strong onshore winds it is sensible to postpone the approach until the cold front has passed bringing clear air and a veer of wind, but in moderate weather it will usually suffice to make the landfall on a conspicuous feature that can be identified from a safe position in deep water.

97

A shift of wind accompanying a deterioration in weather can mean very different things to boats in the same area and point to the way strategy may be adapted to turn them to advantage. A vessel near Land's End with the wind freshening and veering NW with the passage of a cold front could have the inhospitable north coast of Cornwall for a lee shore if she is bound north, while another bound up Channel would find a fair wind and the shelter of a weather shore. For those who have an eye to the changes of the weather and their own advantage these things are not accidental.

10

PREPARING FOR HEAVY WEATHER

Heavy weather is an expression which is apt to conjure up the vision of huge breaking seas and clouds of spindrift driven by gale force winds in which the yacht and her crew can no longer pursue the aim of reaching their destination but have to devote all their energy to the single immediate goal of survival. Such conditions occur but rarely in summer in the waters of NW Europe and seldom last more than a few hours, moreover they take many hours to develop and never occur without visible warning even on the rare occasions when the forecast underestimates the wind strength. A yacht making ocean passages is likely to experience prolonged blows from time to time and has no alternative other than to endure them, but a yacht that is within a day's sail of the land may have to consider her plans very carefully on the approach of heavy weather if she is to avoid being caught close to a lee shore or among tiderips or shoals.

The threshold of heavy weather for a given yacht might be defined as the state of wind and sea that so inhibit her operation that her mode of handling is dictated by weather conditions rather than by the original aims of her crew. Many factors beside wind strength will determine these conditions, but the skipper will probably come to use wind strength as a convenient yardstick and become alert for trouble at a particular figure on the Beaufort Scale. Other factors are the strength and ability of the crew (including himself), the seaworthiness of the yacht, and local geography.

The first realization that you are in for whatever fits your definition of heavy weather is apt to arouse an inner clamour that may drown the voice of reason and lead to confusion of aim and action unless the practical needs of the situation have been thought out beforehand. The first essential is to review your aims and strategy. You need time for this, so marshall the facts and probabilities at once and then brood on them while the rest of your crew are busy making the practical preparations.

The first fact you need to know is where you are, so bring the EP plot up to date and get the best fix you can. Next assemble all you know about the weather situation, not merely the latest forecast but everything that you have observed and the tendencies revealed by the reports from coastal stations. This will enable you to fill out the picture given by the forecast and perhaps add precision to its terms.

If you do not know any of the refuges that are within reach—

It is a good plan to make a time scale and fill in a programme of all known or foreseeable events. For instance, if the weather is associated with the passage of the frontal troughs of a depression and you expect the warm front to pass through your position in four to six hours and the cold front seven hours later you can enter these events against your estimated times. You should also enter other relevant events such as the turning of tidal streams, rising and setting of sun and moon, and also positions that you could expect to reach at various times. It will then be easy to see whether it is possible to reach a port whose approach needs a minimum visibility of four miles before the arrival of the warm sector reduces visibility below this limit, and also what your position could be when the cold front brings a major veer of wind in about twelve hours' time. As time passes you can revise this programme with fresh information and reduce some of the uncertainties. Thus the news on a coastal station report that the barometer stopped falling at Scilly at a certain time might enable you to improve on your estimate of the time at which to expect the warm front off the Casquets.

This graphic construction of a developing picture of the situation helps to dispel the uncertainties that are the main cause of lack of confidence and anxiety and is a great aid to decision making especially if any emergency should arise.

The first question you need to answer is whether to stick to your original aim, remain at sea with a different plan, or seek

—a large harbour that is used by big ships is likely to be the best

shelter. The time-honoured and seamanlike manoeuvre of 'getting the Hell out of here' has powerful attractions and makes good sense if you can be sure of gaining shelter before deteriorating visibility and worsening weather render the exercise unwise. If you are familiar with the bolt hole you will know under what conditions you can make it, if not you must try and work it out. Is there a tide race or shoal water in the approach? Is the entrance completely exposed or can you expect even a partial lee? What minimum visibility is needed to pick up the marks? If you make a mistake can you get out of trouble? What conditions can you expect at your estimated time of arrival? If you do not know any of the refuges that are within your reach, a large harbour that is used by big ships is likely to be the best bet. The entrance will probably be wider, deeper and better marked than a small place; it is also likely to be charted on a bigger scale and be more fully described in the *Pilot*. However, if you have done your passage planning thoroughly you will not be unprepared at this stage.

If there is a chance that entry to any available refuge will be dangerous by the time you can get there you will have no alternative but to remain at sea, maybe for longer than you had anticipated. The first task is to try and form a picture of the way in which the weather will develop along your intended track. You may as well carry on towards your destination, but allowing for the possibility that winds may exceed those forecast and force you to lie a-try or even run off, will any expected wind shifts leave you adequate sea room? In rough weather you want to keep well clear of shipping routes because both visibility and your own freedom to manoeuvre will be restricted. These considerations may persuade you to alter course and head for a suitable position in which to ride it out clear of the land and traffic until the worst is over, and if there is no urgency to increase your offing you may as well anticipate the need to reduce sail so that any further reduction is rendered as simple as possible.

During the time that you have spent brooding over the chart and the forecasts you will have roused your crew into action aimed at making life less unpleasant for them in the future. First consult the cook. If the crew have not recently had a hot meal it could be a good idea to prepare one before things get too rough and at the same time organize some siege rations so that less cooking will be required later. Get the crew to carry out all routine maintenance tasks that are going to become due and any outstanding repairs that ought not to be left. Have them check all stowages on deck and below, doubling up on lashings where necessary and making sure that there will be no need for anyone to go climbing about the decks to grapple with inadequately secured gear. All the openings in the hull, hatches, scuttles, navel pipe, ventilators, seacocks, should be closed if not required to be open, and a note taken of those remaining open. Additional lifelines may be rigged on deck if appropriate and preparations made for shortening sail or setting storm canvas, making sure that all rarely-used items of gear are accessible and serviceable.

Finally, when all is combat-ready, stand down everyone you can spare, and while you relax over a drink or that hot meal discuss the situation, explaining your intentions and giving any necessary instructions.

11

COOKING AT SEA

It is 2015 on a leaden summer evening in the English Channel. Three yachts are bashing close-hauled under shortened sail into a pig of a sea. All are expecting the strong sou'westerly to veer and moderate as a depression passes north of Scotland, and for better conditions to prevail by dawn. They do not yet know that a newly-formed secondary will pull the wind back to the south and that the midnight forecast will threaten them with 'south to southwest 5 to 7 locally 8. Rain. Moderate becoming poor.'

On board *Shadrach* the watch has just been relieved. Those coming off have taken off their oilskins and settled themselves as comfortably as they can in corners of the saloon settees for their evening meal, a hot, appetizing risotto made with rice, ham, peas, nuts and sultanas in a single pan and which they eat with spoons from bowls. After the risotto comes fresh fruit, and then—unexpected touch of luxury—café calypso. The relieving watch have already eaten and are established in the cockpit as comfortably as the dismal weather will allow, a good meal under their belts, confidence in their hearts. The duty cook has parried the congratulations of the crew by saying truthfully that he has had little to do, and points to the single cooking-pot, wooden spoon, vegetable knife and kettle which are all the tools he has used.

In *Mishak*'s saloon the relieving watch are still partly-dressed awaiting their supper, though one man, struggling with his oilskins, is only too anxious to escape into the fresh air on deck and effect the overdue relief of the watch, his appetite annihilated by the rich aroma of tinned stew. The cook, harassed and exhausted, is trying to ladle out the runny stew, with potatoes and peas, from three saucepans onto plates. Some of the stew has spilt onto the stove-top and burnt. The galley is strewn with saucepan lids, spoons, a sprinkling of peas and fragments of potato. The sink contains opened tins of peaches and custard: it is the safest place for them, and when they are disposed of there will be room for the plates which have been used for the first course. The burning stew has been the last straw for the cook who is feeling seasick but hanging on, grimly determined to finish his job and feed the crew—though he could face none of it himself. His effort is cruelly wasted. Most of his customers toy with the food and put their plates aside unfinished. The relieved watch come below to find their food no longer hot, the cabin disordered and reeking of gravy. They too fail to do justice to the cook's sacrifice, and as night falls *Mishak*'s people are convinced that they are having a miserably rough time.

The skipper of *Abednego* has decided that it is too rough for proper cooking. 'We'll just help ourselves to a snack, and get something hot when the weather improves.' The space between the settee berths is partly filled by a sodden jib. 'We'll bag it when this lot eases up a bit.' A recumbent, anguished form fills one settee, while an oil-skinned figure, propped against the companionway, is eating cheese and raw onions, an ancient and malodorous pipe still crooked in his left thumb. This is the skipper: tough, impervious to seasickness and discomfort alike, he is genuinely astonished that anyone should need to sleep in a dry bed or eat hot food, and is apt to complain of being let down by his crews.

It is easy to picture the conditions aboard these yachts twelve hours later. *Shadrach*'s cook, having done the small amount of clearing up after the evening meal, made hot drinks in vacuum flasks, put out biscuits, dried fruit and chocolate for the night watchkeepers, and turned in to his bunk. For breakfast he made porridge, coffee, and—a concession to the now vile weather— bacon sandwiches. By producing good and suitable food at the right times without drama, he not only gives the crew physical sustenance but psychological reassurance of the ship's ability to operate normally regardless of the weather. *Shadrach* is taking the weather in her stride, as fit to fight on as she was on the previous day and as she will be tomorrow.

In *Mishak*, the galley resembles an abandoned battlefield. Since no-one could face the task of clearing up after supper, the stove is littered with gooey saucepans, and the sink full of unwashed dishes and cutlery. For breakfast, the seasick cook managed to make tea, and those who felt up to it ate biscuits or bread and marmalade. *Mishak* is under siege, her crew are tired, and although she is being properly handled and the gear is sound, organization is slipping, life has become abnormal and so the weather seems to be abnormally bad. Skipper and crew are longing to get into harbour: it seems to them necessary that they should be able to rest and straighten things out before the ship is once again seaworthy.

Everyone aboard *Abednego* would agree that conditions are perfectly normal. Another wet sail, this one damaged, has joined the first on the cabin sole, 'No point in putting it away until it's been mended', and an exhausted man still wearing oilskins is asleep spreadeagled on top of the heap, which he found more inviting and easier to get into than his bunk. Since no-one is responsible for catering and cooking at sea, each man helping himself according to inclination, the galley is a bewildering dump of open packets, half-emptied tins and dirty utensils. The crew, spurred by their skipper's hardihood and unquenchable spirit, have coped heroically with a succession of dramas during the night and are surviving. So long as no accident befalls the skipper, and provided that fatigue does not cause him to make any irremediable mistake, *Abednego*'s people will win through to boast of their triumph in many a bar and many a rivetting article in the yachting magazines.

All three yachts weathered the blow. *Shadrach* made her destination in good order the following afternoon, her crew lively enough to go ashore for a drink and a meal, and next morning they were ready to go on. *Mishak* diverted to the nearest harbour where she remained for twenty-four hours recuperating. *Abednego* also reached her destination—the same as *Shadrach*'s—

but much later. One man left the ship immediately with his kit-bag, the remainder slept for ten hours and then stayed in port for four days.

The part played by food in influencing the morale, energy and well-being of a crew is so important, and the time, effort, space and equipment that have to be devoted to its acquisition, stowage, preparation and disposal so great, that the whole subject of catering merits careful thought by the cruising skipper. The preparation, serving and subsequent cleaning-up of meals takes more time and uses more equipment than any other routine activity in the life of a yacht at sea. If the weather is rough, the galley ill-planned, or the yacht badly managed, the task can be as difficult and dangerous as any operation on deck or in the engine-room. The fortunes of the three yachts in our story illustrates how the attitudes of three different skippers and the performances of their cooks affected their crews and the success of their cruises.

Shadrach and her crew were attuned to her function, organized for being at sea. Her menu for the evening meal was well suited to the prevailing circumstances, being both appetizing and nourishing and yet needing only one saucepan and a kettle in its preparation. The entire meal was easy to handle both in preparation, serving, eating and washing up. Cooking smells, so stimulating in harbour and so nauseating to some at sea, were largely eliminated by modifying the recipe. In harbour the cook would have started his risotto by frying the rice together with chopped onion and carrot before adding stock cubes and boiling water; this time he omitted the frying stage altogether, reduced his usual flavourings and added only a few flakes of dried onion. The result was a little more puddingy but none the less welcome to hungry men. The freshness of apples and oranges, the simplest of all desserts, made an excellent complement, while the final touch—coffee with a dash of Tia Maria—not only added a few valuable calories and some stimulus to balance the soporific effect of the rice, but carried faintly exotic overtones and an evocation of plusher and better insulated surroundings. A crew like this that is well organized, led with foresight and intelligently fed, has the best chance of maintaining its energy, has the easiest time in any given set of conditions and—if an emergency should arise—is in the best position to cope with it.

The comparative hardship experienced aboard *Mishak* in the same conditions owed its origin to a lack of flexibility. The menu for her evening meal would have been perfectly suitable in fine weather or in harbour, but on this occasion it put too much strain on the cook and on the galley facilities. The materials of the meal were physically difficult to control, both in the cooking and in the eating, so that the cook was struggling and the meal late. Worst of all the smell and appearance of the food was more than the squeamish could take. Delay in handing over the watch, the unsatisfactory meal, and the lapse from orderliness below undermined the organization and demanded extra effort from the crew in their unsuccessful attempts to prevent things from getting worse. Conscious of having a bad time they were soon in retreat and the skipper's decision to seek shelter was an acknowledgement that his ship and crew were no longer completely seaworthy.

Abednego's troubles arose because she had no real skipper. Her owner, nominally responsible and fully qualified in terms of knowledge and ability, was really a single-hander manqué, a man temperamentally more fitted to sail alone who, lacking the imagination and resourcefulness to manage by himself, depended on the help of others. Hardy by nature and indifferent to discomfort, he could see only weakness in those not similarly endowed, and his eventful cruises were characterized by the brilliant extrication of the yacht from difficulties she need never have encountered. The danger in this situation is that because the crew are never allowed to be more than coolies (and inefficient coolies at that because their welfare is neglected), the safety of the ship depends entirely upon one man.

The galley arrangements in a cruising yacht need not be elaborate, but if the cook is to be able to do his job at sea, these must meet three essential conditions. The first is that the cook must be physically secure while working with both hands: if he has to hold on with one hand while working he is not only under an unreasonable handicap but is exposed to the risk of injury. The second is that there must be a safe place for him to put down hot pans and other items. The third is that the galley must be properly lit and ventilated when the ship is battened down in rough weather. Once these requirements have been met it is very much a question of balancing personal preference against the space available and the depth of one's pocket, but two items of equipment confer such great advantages as to deserve high priority: these are a gymballed stove and a pressure cooker. The gymballed stove almost merits essential rating—especially when there is no other gymballed surface such as the cabin table—but the fact is that many people manage without one, relying on good fiddles or pan clamps to hold pots over the flame when heeled. The pressure cooker saves time, enables one pot to do the work of two or more, and retains its contents regardless of attitude. Perhaps the surest way to a well-equipped galley is for the skipper to take his share of cooking when on passage.

More than any other member of the crew, the cook needs information about what is going on, about what is likely to happen and the skipper's plans in general. In all but the largest and most lavishly equipped yachts, the management of catering is affected by all sorts of conditions both long and short term: the order in which perishable stores are to be used; the crew's output of energy; the state of sea and weather; and variations of routine. For instance, if the normal routine is to have a cold snack at lunch and a cooked meal in the evening, and during the forenoon the skipper knows that the sea is likely to become much rougher by evening, he might acquaint the cook with the fact and discuss whether to switch the meals round. If the skipper intends to enter harbour within an hour or two of a normal mealtime and is sure of being able to carry out his intention, there is a good case (especially if the weather is bad) for postponing the meal so that all can eat together in comfort and peace. Except in an emergency, it should never happen that the cook announces a meal only to be told by the skipper, 'just hold on to it for half-an-hour, I want all hands on deck'. Either the work on deck should be completed in time for the meal, or the cook should be given adequate warning of the intended postponement.

In the same way the skipper should encourage the cook to keep him fully in the picture. When cruising it is always best to buy stores when the opportunity arises rather than to be forced on a particular day to go into a port where stores are available, perhaps having to make a detour or waste a fair wind or tide. If the cook says that it will be necessary to shop and top up with fresh water before the weekend, the skipper's freedom of action remains relatively unrestricted and there is a good chance of being able to perform these chores in a place that is pleasant to visit, thereby enhancing the enjoyment of the cruise. If however the cook says he must get this, that and the other thing tomorrow the skipper must either go to the nearest place where this is possible or do without.

12

KEEPING OUT OF TROUBLE

When suddenly confronted by unexpected danger different people behave in a variety of ways. Some respond with animal signals of warning and alarm, a few display what we call 'presence of mind', instantly producing the right action as though by intuition, while the majority of us do the wrong thing or nothing at all and then kick ourselves for being slow-witted dolts. We surprise ourselves. Normally dependable, not given to panic, in an emergency we seem to suffer a mental disconnection so that we freeze into a state of inertia in which we either stand and gape or else go right on doing whatever happens to occupy us at the time in dogged pursuit of an aim that has lost relevance.

Perhaps an instinct inherited from our forest-dwelling ancestors causes us to congeal at the threat of danger in the same way that modern hedgehogs, living in a countryside that now includes roads, curl into a defensive ball at the approach of any kind of danger. Whatever the reason we must find a way to free ourselves from this paralysis and recover the flexibility to riposte with speed and accuracy. One way to do this is to become so familiar with the event that instead of being surprised by it we recognize it at once, know what else to expect and what we have to do. If we can also distinguish an order of priorities and establish a pattern of action that can be adopted almost automatically, we shall have gone far towards downgrading the status of the event as an 'Emergency'. The man who studies the risks, knows what to expect and what to do, and trains himself to handle them becomes capable of dealing with emergencies *in his own sphere* as though they were routine events (though his brain may well congeal on the instant if he is suddenly required to make a speech). The practical examiner who presents you with a task of some urgency and then springs an emergency on you right in the middle of it is not the sadist you think him. Far from revelling in your discomfiture he is using your flexibility of mind and ability to switch priorities as a gauge of your mastery of the subject.

A skipper must have this flexibility; it is the consequence, the outward visible evidence of his mastery; but he must anticipate and make allowance for the lack of it in most members of his crew. This is not to say that he must resign himself to his orders being carried out by shocked zombies, because if a crew is properly and realistically prepared to cope with an emergency the event loses some of its unexpectedness. Not all, because the realization that one of your comrades is in the sea cannot be simulated, so the drills that are worked out to be used in these situations must be simple and above all physical. Actions which have been learnt are never forgotten like words are. How much of what you memorized by rote at about the time you learned to ride a bicycle can you remember now? Yet even if you have not ridden a bicycle for thirty years you could get on one now and ride it.

Whether the aim of a cruise is to win an offshore race, to reach and explore a distant coast, or to potter gently in familiar waters it is unlikely to be achieved if the yacht is sunk, burnt, stranded or stuck in harbour awaiting repairs, or if her crew are swimming, lying in hospital, or walking home.

The immediate effect of an emergency is to force the substitution of a new aim; overcoming the crisis takes priority over all else until it is achieved. Further effects occur if the emergency is not successfully contained. For instance, if a fire occurs the aim of the cruise is temporarily subordinated to the prime requirement to put out the fire, then provided that the crew and the boat are fit to continue, the original aim is resumed. If however the fire is extinguished only after a prolonged struggle during which a crew member is severely burned and the yacht sustains structural damage the aim of the cruise may be eclipsed altogether by the need to reach a hospital and repair facilities.

An emergency may occasionally result in disaster but seldom does so as the direct outcome of a single incident. Apart from natural catastrophes or genuinely unforeseeable accidents like being obliterated by a falling aircraft, disaster usually develops from a spreading network of incidents which generate one another out of the crew's failure to cope with the original one.

In order to minimize the chances of his aims being frustrated by emergency a skipper needs to evaluate the probable risks, take all reasonable precautions to prevent their occurrence, and make contingency plans to cope with the situation should precautions prove unavailing. Throughout this exercise he encounters one major obstacle—the difficulty of maintaining strict realism in a process of reasoning that is largely conjectural. Few people have much first-hand experience of emergencies. The average yachtsman may after a lifetime of cruising have never been in a fire nor had a member of his crew fall overboard, and may have experienced dire anxiety and alarm through proximity of danger from collision and other causes on no more than two or three occasions. Yet it is of the utmost importance that his thinking on all these questions is informed and realistic. To this end he needs an intimate knowledge and understanding of his crew, of his ship and her gear as well as of the circumstances imposed by the nature of his operations. Finally, all drills should be tested and rehearsed under conditions that resemble as far as possible those that might be encountered in a real emergency. Every cruise, every ship and each individual crew member is different, there are no reach-me-down all-purpose solutions and no short cuts to a guaranteed trouble-free cruise. We shall examine a number of typical emergencies to illustrate the method of approaching the problem and not by any means with the intention of establishing any model answer because that can only be done with reference to real people with real intentions in real boats.

In assessing risks the first step towards realism is to admit that a risk exists, and the second is to recognize that some element of risk has to be accepted if the aim is to be achieved. The pretence that all risk can and should be eliminated is counter to all experience of our own everyday behaviour and leads to muddled and misleading thinking.

Some of the more obvious hazards to be guarded against are

injuries consequent on falls, burning and scalding, accidents with gear; disabling illness; one or more members of the crew falling overboard; fire and explosion; the vessel being damaged by collision with other ships, flotsam or fixed objects; stranding; heavy weather damage. The list seems formidable and might in some circumstances be extended, but we need not be daunted by it because the actual risk, which is no greater at sea than it is on shore for many of the items, can be greatly reduced by forethought and preparation.

Knocks, bumps and burns

More cruises are marred by injury to crew members than any other cause. Assessment of the risk begins with individuals: the very old and the very young, the unfit or handicapped are particularly vulnerable, as are those whose normal performance is lowered by cold, fatigue or seasickness. Next to be considered are the boat and her equipment. We look for the potential sources of danger, slippery surfaces, inadequate handholds, sharp corners, fittings and gear that trap fingers or feet. Most of these reveal themselves soon enough so the task does not entail huge feats of the imagination. Consideration of dangerous circumstances need not take much time because we must assume the worst possible conditions, a rapid motion, maximum heel, wet people and surfaces, darkness and haste.

Having studied the risk, the next step is to reduce it. Material considerations being the easiest to deal with, we can start by providing non-slip surfaces and handholds where needed, eliminating or guarding projecting corners, moving or modifying gear where possible, and establishing attachment points for safety harnesses or similar restraints. Some traps may have to remain because the only solution would be a new boat or a major change to the rig, and the only way to reduce the risk from these is to warn the crew of the danger that exists and teach them how to take care of themselves, insisting for example that anyone cooking at sea wears oilskins and waterproof boots as protection against scalding.

Finally, we must provide for the eventuality that despite precautions an accident may occur. This involves much more than having a first-aid kit on board because it is on the skipper's handling of the situation at this point, on his ability to reorganize his intention and his priorities, that the whole future trend of events depends. A mistake at this point may open the way to an avalanche of subsequent incidents leading to eventual disaster. In a case of injury the immediate action is clearly first-aid to the victim followed by a decision on the need for and degree of urgency in seeking skilled attention. In all cases where a crew member becomes a casualty, the identity of the victim and the effect of his loss on the strength of the crew is critical. If a person who is only there as a passenger gets put out of action the skipper's sole problem is the welfare of the patient. The yacht may divert or not according to need without being handicapped beyond the permanent occupation of one berth and perhaps the fairly continual attendance of some member of the crew. On the other hand, if the only experienced and competent member of a weak crew is removed from active participation a whole new set of problems arises. Suppose the skipper in a family crew consisting of his wife and young children breaks some ribs or worse, can the rest cope? If they cannot, what needs to be done in order to safeguard them against this by no means remote possibility? When a crew contains one apparently indispensable member, his loss or disablement ranks as an emergency in its own right and demands that all necessary preparations be made to ensure that the rest of the crew are competent to take over and that the information they need is available and intelligible.

In deciding what needs to be done a 'shopping list' of necessary equipment will emerge as a kind of appendix to the process, and each item of equipment will have to be assigned a stowage, kept in working order and its location and use explained to all the crew.

Seasickness, exposure and dehydration

'No-one ever died of seasickness' may be a true fact but it is a fact that conceals the truth. It tempts the retort, 'nor was bitten to death by teredos', for if several members of a crew are disabled by seasickness the vessel may be in as much danger as if each was a worm-riddled plank.

The effects of seasickness extend far beyond the miseries of the sufferer. Depending on the degree of his affliction, a seasick man may be unreliable, unable to work or incapable of doing anything for himself, so that another must not only do his work for him but look after him as well. Add to this the disruption to the domestic arrangements in the average small yacht caused by the permanent occupation of one or more bunks, and the crew are severely handicapped.

Almost nobody is immune. Some may meet the conditions that set them off more rarely than others and some may recover entirely after a short bout, but the only certain remedy is 'to go and sit under a tree'—in other words the cessation of motion. Prevention is therefore a matter for everyone and each should use his own experience to add detail to the broad principles which seem to have general application.

General physical fitness is an advantage and those of sedentary habit would do well to get more fresh air and exercise than usual in the fortnight or so before going to sea. Diet has a direct bearing on resistance to seasickness. Before sailing eat and drink in sensible moderation and at sea avoid rich, indigestible or highly flavoured food. Frequent light snacks at intervals of one to three hours are better than larger meals at conventional times, and everyone should be encouraged to nibble something whenever he begins to feel empty. If a person begins to look preoccupied, changes colour or becomes unusually quiet, he is probably in need of nourishment, occupation, warmth or fresh air. He will seek the last of his own accord, but may need some urging before he will eat anything: a plain dry biscuit is often effective in retrieving a potential victim from the brink. Make sure he is warm enough and give him a job such as steering that will absorb his attention but does not require violent exertion. Sooner or later he will have to go below in order to rest and although the reeling cabin may be the last straw, a good sleep in a warm bunk is best for him and with luck he may wake up to find his sea-legs.

Drugs are wonderfully effective but need to be used carefully. Some seasickness remedies cause overpowering drowsiness in certain individuals and everyone needs to find out for himself what type suits him and causes least side-effects. A crew man may get round this by taking an anti-seasickness pill when he goes off watch and sleeping it off, but a skipper who is susceptible to side-effects must either find a drug that is free of them or do without. All anti-seasickness pills are more effective if a preliminary dose is taken the night before sailing and many people have reported that this practice reduces the stupefying effects of subsequent doses.

The loss of fluid and the depletion of energy due to starvation in seasickness may cause dehydration and increase the risk of exposure and hypothermia. Some of the symptoms of dehydration, dizziness, fatigue, weakness and a tendency to faint, are usual in severe seasickness and suggest that part of a seasick person's sufferings are caused by it. The danger of dehydration lies in the reduction in the volume of the blood and in its water and salt content, which can result in severe shock following quite minor injury. In the incipient stage of seasickness it is best to eat dry food and avoid drinking (though a person who is nauseated by anything else can often drink Oxo), but once the vomiting stage has been reached the patient should be encouraged to drink a mouthful or two of plain water at intervals.

Most sufferers recover with such alacrity on reaching smooth water that the sympathy of their shipmates is apt to evaporate in doubt as to the genuineness of the affliction, but if anyone fails to show signs of recovery within a very short time his symptoms are not attributable solely to motion sickness and he should be seen by a doctor.

Exposure is a subject that is usually associated with mountain climbing, arctic travel, falling overboard and shipwreck, but anyone who cruises in NW European waters in winter or spring or goes north of 58° latitude at any season will find that in bad weather he and his crew have to contend with it.

The lowering of the core-temperature of the body progressively inhibits mental and physical performance, and if unchecked is quickly fatal. Symptoms are shivering, muscular inco-ordination and weakness beginning with the hands, apathy and confusion, sluggishness of thought and speech; the hands become inoperative, movement of other limbs is accomplished with increasing difficulty until eventually the victim can neither walk nor stand, shivering stops, the subject becomes irrational and incoherent. Unconsciousness occurs when the body temperature falls to about 80°F (66°C) and death can be expected one or two hours later.

Body heat is lost by conduction to any material in contact with the body, especially water whose thermal conductivity is two hundred times that of air, radiation from exposed skin, convection, and evaporation from skin and lungs. It is retained naturally by constriction of surface blood vessels, and artificially by wearing clothes and heating the environment. Lost heat is replaced from the body's energy reserves which it derives from food, by conduction from hot food and drink and exposure to external sources of heat like the sun and hot-water bottles.

Exposure is an obvious threat to the life of a swimmer, but you do not need to fall overboard to suffer from it. Thanks to the effect of wind chill the man who gets soaked to the skin on a cool summer night, say 50°F (19°C), only needs to be exposed to a twenty knot wind to suffer the equivalent of a freezing temperature. Wet and without the protection of clothes his useful life would be about fifteen minutes. No-one in his senses would be on deck naked in these conditions but unless he is really well protected against wind and water he could quickly become inefficient and by the end of his watch might even need treatment.

Prevention is essentially the restriction of heat loss by wearing warm wind-and-waterproof clothing, remembering that head and hands are particularly significant areas; maintenance of energy reserves by eating high-calorie food at frequent intervals. Alcohol should be avoided because it dilates the blood vessels of the skin and although this produces a sensation of warmth it actually promotes heat loss.

Treatment aims at preventing further heat loss and raising the body temperature. If the patient is still feeling very cold, is shivering and has not reached the stage of collapse it will usually suffice to remove him from the reach of wind and weather, exchange wet clothes for dry ones, get him to lie down in a sleeping-bag and give some warm food or drink. If he is collapsed *he will be unable to warm himself* no matter how well he is wrapped up and his temperature could continue to fall, so an external source of heat must be provided. One of the most effective methods is for someone to get into the sleeping-bag alongside him if there is a big enough bunk, otherwise hot-water bottles can be used, taking care not to burn the patient who should be watched for signs that the treatment is effective. If it is not, more heat must be applied, and eventually mouth-to-mouth resuscitation may be necessary. Do not allow anyone to give alcohol to the patient; it could be fatal.

Avoiding collision

We all started practising collision avoidance when we first began to crawl and have been adding daily to our experience ever since, so that by the time we come to do it at sea we already know a great deal about it. Why then does it present such a problem?

There are three separate steps in the process of avoiding collision. These are:

1 Detecting the presence of your opponent.
2 Assessing relative motion and determining whether a collision threat exists.
3 Adjusting your own motion to maintain an avoiding path.

Detection must be made early enough to allow time for the second and third actions. Failure may occur for the following reasons either singly or in combination:

1 Inefficient look-out.
2 Blind sectors caused by the vessel's structure or rig.
3 Poor visibility.
4 Small size of target making it impossible to see until too late or it enters a blind sector.
5 Distraction of attention by more obvious or pressing matters.

When the other vessel has been detected its relative motion is very easily judged provided both vessels maintain constant course and speed, and avoiding action is usually slight and easy to achieve if taken early. The closer the vessels approach one another the more drastic is the avoiding action needed and the less chance of correcting any mistake. The steering and sailing rules in IRPCS are designed to remove uncertainty as to which vessel should give way and to make the likely action of each predictable to the other. (For lack of such rules pedestrians sometimes confront one another harmlessly in a comic little dance which would be neither harmless nor comic if they were ships.)

A small yacht is at a disadvantage through being a very insignificant object, especially in a rough sea, and may escape the notice of a large vessel who may well be concerning herself with the movements of several other ships much further away from her than the yacht. Commonsense says that the yacht should take advantage of her superior manoeuvrability to give way although the rules enjoin her to hold her course and speed, but this must be done with discretion because you cannot tell whether you have been seen or not, and if the ship alters course to give way at about the same time as you do the collision situation may remain with the added hazard that now neither of you knows what to expect the other to do next. If, having established that the two vessels are on a collision course or that you are likely to cross ahead of the other vessel by only a small margin, you decide it is prudent to alter course to pass astern of her you should watch her very carefully in case she alters as well, and continue to take bearings to ensure that you will pass clear.

All watch leaders ought to know the IRPCS well enough to be able to interpret lights and shapes and to anticipate the actions of other vessels. They should also be capable of estimating relative motion and of recognizing the existence of a collision risk. The standing orders which the skipper lays down about collision avoidance will be based on the competence of his watch leaders, so the more he can teach them the less often will they need to call him out, and these must ensure that if a situation requires his presence on deck he must be given enough time to size it up.

In practice a single vessel in open water and good visibility rarely causes difficulty. It is when crossing streams of traffic that problems arise and on such occasions most skippers do well to take over the deck themselves.

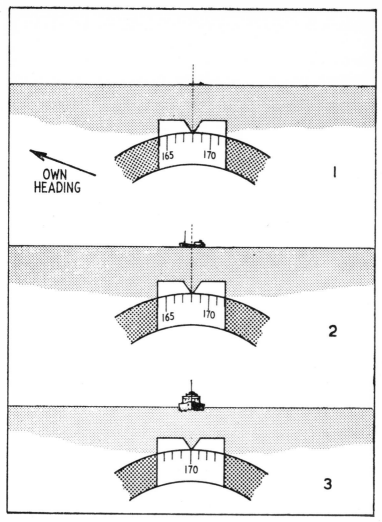

OWN
HEADING

1

2

3

Ship on a constant bearing (1 and 2): collision is inevitable unless
one vessel alters course or speed; (3) ship has altered course and will
pass clear if the bearing continues to increase

The best protection against collision is a good lookout all
round the horizon. The next is to be conspicuous, a correctly
mounted radar reflector, and by night really bright navigation
lights. Remember that a ship that is apparently going clear may,
if she has not seen you, endanger you by altering course to avoid

another. If you suspect that a ship on a collision course has not seen you turn away and use white flares or shine a powerful white torch at the bridge. Floodlighting the sails is much less effective at a distance than it is from your own deck; it may not be noticed or may cause incomprehension and delay response.

Fire

The trouble with fire in a boat is that if you are going to fight it you have to remain in the arena with it. On land, if the fire gets too hot you can stand back and throw water at it from a distance or at least save your skin by running away. At sea you have either got to put it out very quickly or opt for a different sort of risk by taking to the liferaft, which is a very poor life-support system compared with even a disabled yacht.

The priorities in respect of the fire hazard are distinct. They are:

1 Take all possible steps to minimize the chances of an outbreak.

2 If fire does occur make certain of putting it out quickly otherwise it is unlikely to be put out at all. Extinguishers must be capable of being brought into action at once and be quickly effective.

3 While firefighting complete preparations for abandoning ship. There may not be time when the decision is made.

The first step in minimizing the risks is to list all the factors that contribute to the fire hazard, and to write opposite each one the action that you can take to eliminate or reduce it. Some of the risk-producing factors can be neutralized altogether and others mitigated so that only the odd one remains. In the example on page 140 two of these factors are the presence on board of liquefied gas and petrol. The hazard can be greatly reduced by substituting paraffin and diesel but unless the auxiliary and the cooking stove need replacing anyway you would probably settle for precautions against leaks and accumulations of vapour, with meticulous observance of sound installation practices and operating routines. The precautions then divide themselves into those that can be taken care of once and for all and those that have to be exercised more or less continuously. Among these last there are likely to be a few dos and don'ts or standing orders which should be kept few and simple and scrapped the moment you are no longer prepared to enforce them.

Allowing that your precautions may be inadequate and that there is a point beyond which they become absurd or intolerable, you have to think how to save the situation. The first products of fire are smoke and among modern materials some extremely unpleasant fumes which soon incapacitate anyone who inhales them, so having warned the crew they need to be got out on deck together with all the firefighting equipment. Fuel needs to be isolated by closing tank cocks and moving portable containers, and all hatches and scuttles should be kept closed except where the use of extinguishers requires them to be open.

Failure to put the fire out would lead to a distress situation and abandoning ship, so preparations for this eventuality must be made during the firefighting phase. All this forms the substance of a standing order detailing the action to be taken in the event of fire, but much more needs to be thought about and questions answered or at least asked before the event. These concern the handling of the yacht if she is underway so as to reduce the spread of flames and the hampering effects of smoke; whether it is better to beach her so that help of shore firefighters can be enlisted or to remove her from the chance of setting fire to other vessels and shoreside property. Such points are primarily the concern of the skipper, but although they may profitably be discussed with the rest of the crew they should not be included in any drills or standing orders because the introduction of numerous conditions would complicate them and destroy their value.

Man overboard

Imagine that you have just fallen overboard. Well why not? Since when did the rank of skipper confer immunity? Suddenly you are underwater, frantically barricading your lungs against the sea and struggling towards the light and air, your whole future hanging on the thoroughness with which you and your crew have prepared for this moment. Surfacing, the sea seems rougher than it did from on deck and empty. EMPTY! Good God, where's the yacht? Suppressing the surge of panic you turn slowly round and see the upper part of mast and sails, a halyard streaming from the masthead. How far away she is, and still going. Has anyone seen? Yes. For a moment you glimpse activity on deck as you and the boat rise coincidentally to the crests, and in the same instant there is a lifebuoy on the opposite slope of the trough. It is drifting downwind. Get to it quickly before you have to chase it. Swimming in all those clothes is exhausting, like running in soft sand, and when you finally reach the lifebuoy you are breathless and in need of a rest, so you capsize it over your head in the approved manner, hook your arms over it and lie there gasping.

After a time you recover enough to raise your head and see the yacht returning. The jib that you were in the middle of hoisting when you fell in has been pulled down, but its halyard still trails aloft, snaking and swaying. Now she is fifty yards away, showing her weather side as she heads for a point downwind of you to luff and pick you up. You see the figures on deck, intent faces turned in your direction; one of them waves. Now she is end on, head-to-wind, mainsail flogging, spray bursting against her bow. But you have only ever practised this manoeuvre in sheltered water and she undershoots, losing way a length downwind. Someone throws a line but it was badly coiled and the tangle caught by the wind falls ten feet out on the beam. Shouts, foredeck hand hurriedly recovering the rope, the boat drifting back slowly paying off and all the time the mainsail slatting and flogging. A burst of sound from the exhaust quickly muted, a pause, a few beats of the exhaust under power and then silence, even the sail is quiet for a moment. As the grey backs of intervening seas interrupt your view of the receding yacht you realize that no-one is looking in your direction any more.

Up to now you have been able to keep facing downwind towards the yacht by paddling with your hands, but now your arms stretched out horizontally across the lifebuoy are stiffening, pain seizes your shoulder joints and you realize that you are very cold.

Instinctively your body wants to draw your arms in to your sides and across your chest to reduce the radiating area and the loss of heat, and for a while you fidget around trying to huddle into a ball without losing your hold on the lifebuoy, but the best you can manage is to hook both arms in front of you over one rim. In this strained position with your weight all on one side of the buoy, your face is so low in the water that you have trouble in breathing; so you revert to hanging on winged-out arms in the attitude which the Romans knew to be fatal even on dry land. How you wish you had on a good buoyancy jacket that would keep you afloat with just an arm through one of the lifebuoy's lanyards. Even more you wish that you had worn a safety harness and remained on board.

You surmise that after the first abortive attempt to pick you up, your crew started the engine but got the propellor fouled in a line trailing overboard, a jib sheet most probably. She wouldn't handle too well under mainsail alone, they'd need to get a jib on her and that would mean retrieving the halyard. You wouldn't have let them waste time on that; if they failed to recover it quickly you'd have made them unreeve it so that it couldn't foul things up and use the spinnaker halyard instead. But why did they never get the mainsail to draw? The upper part of the rig is still visible and when the passing crests swing you round in the right direction you can see the sail fluttering still. They must have got a major snarl-up there. Wonder what it can be . . .

Your next view of the yacht shows the mainsail set into a taut purposeful curve, the mast steady and leaning, and a white ribbon of jib climbing the forestay. Strangely, you are not elated at this sign of renewed hope for you are now stupefied by cold, your face has become a rigid mask, your limbs tremble violently, the agony in your shoulders is complemented by cramp in your calves, and the uncontrollable gasps by which you are now breathing inhale air and water indiscriminately.

The yacht approaches in short tacks, a figure in the pulpit scanning anxiously ahead. Suddenly he sees you, for an arm shoots out and he calls aft to the cockpit. If you were not so far gone you would be terrified because this time she is going too

125

fast. You know there will be a line and you know that your hands are incapable of grasping it. Mercifully it falls right across you and with an enormous effort you achieve a clumsy screwing movement of your right arm which puts two full turns of the line round the forearm, then you double the arm across your chest and clamp it with the other. The strain comes on with a wrench that nearly dislocates your shoulder and pulls you under, and as the water covers your head you pass out.

For you, drifting in and out of consciousness, half full of water and three parts dead, bumping up and down against the smooth hard hull, time has stopped and space has shrunk to the length of your arm: you feel the clutch of hands, see faces made grotesque with effort swoop into close-up and out of sight, but the deck so safely supporting the owner of the hand that grips your collar is as inaccessible to you as the moon.

For those on deck, faced with the task of getting your water-logged carcase back aboard and re-animating it, the next quarter of an hour was a nightmare. They had recognized that there would be a problem but had not grasped the reality. There were two men and a woman, aggregating between them enough strength to lift you out but unable to get hold of you all at the same time for lack of space on the side deck. Having secured a line to the lifebuoy, they then saw that they would have to cut away the guard rails and did so. Next they reviewed the various methods that had been proposed in discussion. Using a boarding-ladder was rejected as pure desktop seamanship, even had it been possible to keep it rigged in that sea it could have caused you severe injury and you were in any event incapable of climbing it. The weather was just too coarse to allow the inflatable to be launched, though it was agreed that in moderate conditions this would have been the quickest means of ensuring your immediate safety because one person could have dragged you into it.

They tried scooping you up in the bunt of a sail but this was soon abandoned as a waste of time. The wind took charge of the sail which was only with difficulty persuaded to enter the water and then showed an obdurate determination to get itself over rather than under you. Bights of rope and bowlines were tried but the sea sucked them away or thrust you away from them, and in the end they had perforce to lasso you with running bowlines, one apiece, and drag you over the side by brute force like a bullock from a bog.

Having recovered from this nasty experience it surprises no-one that you start a one-man crusade to treat the man-overboard hazard a great deal more seriously. Prevention naturally takes your attention first; you pinpoint the occasions of special risk and become much more fussy about the use of safety harnesses. Recognizing that you cannot completely eliminate the risk and that someone (perhaps more than one and not necessarily from your own ship) may go overboard, you define the aims:

1 *Detection* Falling overboard unnoticed is the worst possible start. One timely scream is better than any number of gritted teeth. But what of the man on watch alone?

2 *Keeping in sight* A head at waterlevel is soon lost to view in seaway. (You may not appreciate how soon until you try it in the open sea.) You need a marker to increase the size of the target and a watcher with no other duty than to keep him in sight.

3 *Buoyancy* External support saves energy and heat-loss, reassures the victim and can double as a marker.

4 *Speed of recovery* Besides the well-known dangers of hypothermia the victim may be injured, unconscious, or using up his energy in keeping afloat. A smart, well-rehearsed manoeuvre can put even a large yacht alongside the casualty in less than two minutes. Speed should be improved by practice; haste and corner-cutting may lead to fatal delay.

5 *Lifting on board* This could prove to be the most difficult part of the operation. If the remainder of the crew lack the strength to drag the casualty aboard, a special technique and perhaps special equipment will have to be devised. There is always a possibility that more than one person could go overboard at the one time.

6 *Medical treatment* Some degree of shock and exposure is to

127

be expected. The need for resuscitation is quite likely. If exposure is severe or there are complicating factors like injury, the patient may need treatment beyond the resources of the yacht. Points to be considered are how long it will take to reach medical aid, the feasibility of transferring the patient to lifeboat or helicopter. Only if the patient's life is in danger should you make distress signals, otherwise 'W' by the most suitable means is appropriate.

These aims will generate many trains of thought which will be useless unless strictly realistic. Experiment is necessary not only to test ideas, but to identify problems. You can work out a beautiful man-overboard drill which goes like clockwork in smooth water and force 3 or 4, but if someone falls in while you are running with a bit too much sail in force 6 or more in the open sea, there will be problems for which you are quite unprepared. So sometime when it occurs to you how nasty it would be to fall in at that moment, throw in a marker and see how well your drill works. It is important to use something that does not drift with the wind, best of all would be a ballasted life-sized human dummy that would present you with all the problems including how to get it back aboard, but a lifebuoy or fender will do if it is attached to something like a large coil of rope to act as a drogue. Remember that what you do must be effective under all imaginable circumstances. Landmarks are the easiest aids to orientation, but you cannot count on them being always visible. Gybing is the quickest way back on most points of sailing, but is only acceptable if those remaining on board are capable of gybing that particular yacht in any weather, by day or night, without injury, damage, disorientation or a snarl-up.

The right manoeuvre is of course the one that achieves the right result, but the standard RYA Dayboat drill is a very good example to look at because it satisfies all the requirements of a drill. In this method the helmsman's first action is to turn immediately onto a square reach without tacking; as soon as he has gained enough room he tacks onto the opposite square reach; then, depending on the individual boat and attendant circumstances, he bears away to make the position from which he luffs to a stop alongside the man in the water. Notice that:

1   The helmsman's immediate response is the same regardless of the point of sailing when the victim fell in.

2   This response does not require any sail handling, so no matter how small the crew there is no conflict of priorities to delay the throwing of the lifebuoy and the look-out starting duty.

3   Orientation, which is often a source of difficulty in times of stress, is by apparent wind direction alone. This avoids any need to read the compass and do sums in one's head which will quite likely be wrong.

4   Sail trim is not critical at any time, the only essential action being the freeing of the jibsheet on tacking and an eye to the mizzen if there is one.

5   After tacking, the casualty will be almost dead ahead so if he is lost to view while in stays he can be looked for and found in a small arc.

6   The speed, and therefore the time, is the same on both the outward and inward legs, thus the starting point can be regained even if the casualty has been lost sight of. This last point should be exploited by having someone note the elapsed time. If there is no-one to spare for this the look-out, who has no need to speak since he can indicate direction by pointing, can count off the seconds.

7   Darkness requires no changes to be made in the drill, as a torch capable of illuminating the burgee would be in the cockpit anyway.

The foregoing procedure depends on immediate action by the remaining crew. When one person is alone on deck he may, if he is a single-hander, decide to accept the risk that falling overboard could be the end of his voyage, but if there are others aboard they must not be put in the situation of finding their shipmate gone and of having to start a search. This could mean devising the release of a marker, the sounding of an alarm and stopping the boat;

the same mechanism that released the marker possibly serving to let fly the jib sheet so that the boat would luff and the watch below be alerted by the change of gait and the flogging sails.

A question that crops up regularly is, 'why waste all that time sailing round in a figure eight? If your aim is to get back to the chap as quickly as you can, isn't it better to start the engine and motor straight back to him?' The answer quite simply is that if by using the engine you can effect a speedier rescue then it is the right thing to do. But use of the engine could lead to disastrous delay unless certain things are kept very firmly in mind. The first is that if you are under sail and then try to manoeuvre under power, you must either lower the sails or compete with their effect on the handling characteristics of the yacht. Your approach under power alone to a man in the water would be very different to your approach under sail, but if sail is set it dictates your approach path even though you may be motoring. The second is that since there will be lines in the water there is a distinct advantage in being able to manoeuvre without using a propeller. The third and most important point is that a turning propeller is such an appalling danger to anyone in the water alongside that it is essential to stop the engine before there is any possibility of him being minced. Try it sometime. You must in any event develop the skill to carry out the evolution under sail; time yourself and then try again using the engine, except in very light weather you will need more skill, a deeper understanding of interacting forces. How did the time compare? What discoveries did you make?

In practising the drill there are pitfalls to be guarded against. These arise chiefly from not having a real person in the water but some comparatively small object that is naturally retrieved by a boathook. This would be a highly unsuitable and dangerous implement to use on a man, but since it is in use the man in charge of it is impelled for some reason to take it forward into the bows, and this in turn leads the helmsman to try and bring the boat up so that the object is within his reach. In other words the practice casualty is approached as though he were a mooring buoy. The way to approach a man in the water is to lose way (head-to-

wind if you are under sail) with him abeam of your lowest freeboard and better ten feet away than underneath the boat. Bringing him to the bow unsights him from the helmsman and exposes
him to the danger of being overrun or struck by the pitching
stem. Either could cost his life. Similarly, if the practice is
habitually concluded by whisking a lightweight dummy over the
side the crew may be deluded into believing that they can handle
the incident, while in fact they have never faced up to the task of
recovering a waterlogged and possibly helpless man. No simulated
event can ever be completely realistic; however hard you try the
best you can achieve is a judicious estimate of its relationship to
actuality, but it is better and easier to make this estimate on the
basis of practical experiment than it is on theory alone.

A training establishment might find it worthwhile going to the
considerable trouble of making up a realistic human dummy in
order to practise the whole man-overboard routine in any conditions they choose, but the ordinary yachtsman may well have to
split up the exercise so that the recovery phase is carried out using
a live 'victim' in sheltered water, possibly even at anchor.
This would at least reveal some of the difficulties and test their
solutions. Imaginatively applied, the experiment could go a long
way towards closing the gap between it and reality.

Having decided what you are going to do the next consideration is the equipment you need in order to do it. Restraints,
markers, buoyancy, throwing lines, lifting gear, the list is
formidable and includes not only the provision of each item but
its stowage and maintenance. Various authorities can and do
recommend, even require, a minimum scale of equipment, but it
is up to you as skipper to decide your needs in the light of your
aims. You will find that both the authorities and manufacturers
suffer to some extent from your own main handicap—a dearth of
operational experience and a lack of feedback. The man who
survives is, in his relief, prone to overlook defects of methods and
equipment while the best-informed critics are silent forever in
Davy Jones's locker.

13

EMERGENCY REPAIRS

If a yacht on passage sustains damage that affects her ability to remain afloat or to proceed on her way under control her crew must rely on their own skills and the material resources of their ship to make her seaworthy enough to reach port. The skipper has the additional task of repairing his plans.

All kinds of damage can occur in the quietest of weather but it is more likely to happen when the vessel and her crew are under heavy pressure from strong winds and rough seas, so plans to cope with it must make allowance for the extra difficulty and increased risk of the secondary damage that this will cause.

The immediate aim must be to prevent loss of life or injury to the crew, to keep the boat afloat and to eliminate the risk of secondary damage. In practice the actions will run simultaneously.

Preventing casualties
Warn everyone of the damage. A man who rushes on deck in response to a vague shout or the sound of crashing gear could well go straight over the side if most of his usual handholds have disappeared, the guardrails are slack and the deck is covered in ropes and sails. Check that everyone is on board and uninjured.

Limit the consequences
If you suspect the boat may be making water man the pumps immediately. If holed use any means to slow the intake of water until the pumps can keep her afloat. Reducing speed or a change of heading relative to the seas may relieve the strain on whatever is damaged and ease working conditions. If the rig is damaged,

luff, tack, run off, or reduce sail as appropriate, and if spars are in the water make them fast and get them clear of the hull.

Ascertain the full extent of the damage

Examine the whole boat. The most obvious damage is not necessarily the most serious damage.

Having staved off imminent disaster you can now look further ahead. You need to know how much time is available for repairs, and this in most cases depends on how far you can drift before you hit something, so the first requirement is to fix your position. Unless you are almost ashore there is likely to be more time than you may have thought at first. Use this time to make the hull as watertight as possible and bring the boat under command, preferably under sail because range will then be no problem.

If you cannot set sail you must be ready for the problems that will attend your conversion to a motor boat. If the rig is in the water there will be a mess to clear up before you can do anything else. The drogue effect will reduce your rate of drift but work on deck will be handicapped by the extremely rapid undamped motion of the mastless hull. You will naturally want to salvage as much as possible but make sure everything on deck is well secured and that no ropes' ends can get over the side because a fouled propeller would be crippling. Unless you need to get away from immediate danger it is better not to start the engine until you have decided where to go.

It is easy enough to say where you would like to go, not too difficult to decide which place would be best, but pointless unless you know how *far* you can go. At this point the man who habitually wastes good wind by motoring when he could be sailing can smile smugly because he knows already. The rest of us who only resort to the engine with reluctance and in a flat calm only know how *long*, not how far. We think in terms of gallons per hour which depends more or less on engine speed, but range is a question of miles per gallon which depends on resistance, and so is quite different in a head sea or a headwind to what it is in a calm or with a following wind. Unless you have some figures to go on you must make a very cautious estimate of the range you can get from a given quantity of fuel in other than calm conditions, and if the matter is critical try to measure the actual fuel consumed as you go. The powerful engines of many modern auxiliary yachts enable them to cruise comfortably in calm conditions at power settings lower than that which would give maximum range, but if at this setting speed is much reduced by resistance of rough seas and headwinds the distance covered for a given quantity of fuel (ie range) may be much less than would be achieved if power and speed were increased. The extreme case is that of a boat steaming at low revolutions into a headwind that completely cancels her way. She is using fuel very slowly but getting nowhere and so has maximum endurance but zero range.

With inadequate fuel or an unreliable engine a jury rig must be extemporized out of whatever can be salvaged from the wreck of the rig or cannibalized from the accommodation. This is a major undertaking that could take several days and might involve waiting for a rough sea to moderate. The experience of those who have had to do it seems to indicate that the usual minor spars lashed together can spread a big enough area of sail to give control. The biggest headache is likely to be steadying the jury mast while it is being raised into position, and the construction of a tabernacle to locate the heel of the mast could well take longer than the preparation of the spar itself. The engineless and those who intend to cross oceans (often the same people these days) need to give thought to the ways and means of setting up a jury rig, but for cruising in European waters it is more realistic to study your fuel capacity and engine reliability.

APPENDIX

EVENT	POSSIBLE CAUSES	REMEDY	EMERGENCY ACTION Main points to be included in drills	EQUIPMENT NEEDED
COLLISION	Lack of vigilance Blind areas	Lookout Lookout and eliminate if possible	Warn crew: 'all on deck' Take avoiding action and use appropriate signals to attract attention	Signalling lamp, White flares, Foghorn and whistles
	Inexperienced watchkeepers Unexpected action by other vessels Poor visibility Dense traffic Own vessel inconspicuous	Briefing Be alert. Understand and comply with IRPCS. Get clear of traffic as soon as possible Bright lights. Coloured sails	Put on lifejackets and prepare to abandon If collision unavoidable, try to make it a glancing blow	
FIRE	Careless handling of combustible (including smoking) materials Leakage of volatile fuels Overheating of fuel, lubricating or hydraulic oils Spontaneous combustion (most likely of oily or varnish-soaked rags) Electrical fault	Briefing, discipline and provision of facilities for safe disposal Stick to sound installation and operating practice. Use gas detector Regular inspection and good maintenance routine General cleanliness and order	Warn crew, giving nature and location of the fire. Count all on deck with fire extinguishers Close openings in hull, but ensure none are obstructed If engine running, stop it and isolate fuel Safeguard portable fuel stores, pyrotechnics etc (cans can be put overboard on a line)	Fire-fighting equipment appropriate to size of yacht and types and quantity of fuels on board Gas detector if appropriate Accessible fuel valve

EVENT	POSSIBLE CAUSES	REMEDY	EMERGENCY ACTION Main points to be included in drills	EQUIPMENT NEEDED
FIRE	Fire from an external source	Not a great risk, and not much you can do beyond cultivating general alertness. In certain localities take precautions against lightning	Be prepared to move survival gear out of danger	
MAN OVERBOARD	Carelessness Walking on sails Unsuitable footwear Reaching outboard or upwards while unsecured Urinating or vomiting over the side Violent motion Heavy water on deck Tacking or gybing unexpectedly Slippery decks Lack of handholds Sudden failure of gear (including personal harness and lifelines)	Briefing Use safety harness Always warn crew Rectify Regular inspection and maintenance	Warn crew: 'man overboard' Throw buoyancy/marker Appoint lookout Start whatever manoeuvre you have found effective under all circumstances and which you have practised to perfection Navigator note all clock and compass readings in case a search becomes necessary Make preparations for recovery of victim(s) If other vessels in sight or earshot, signal 'O'	Lifebuoy and light Dan buoy Smoke generator Buoyant line Lifting gear

This table shows how a skipper can review three typical hazards, decide how to reduce them, and what actions and equipment he will need if they occur.